Praise for *The Power of Unpopular*

"Being popular may get you elected to public office, but if you want to be successful in business, you need to understand the power of being unpopular. Erika Napoletano clearly and cleverly lays out the path to unpopularity, a critical new paradigm for business success."

—Carol Roth, Business Strategist and *New York Times* Best-Selling Author of *The Entrepreneur Equation*

"Erika has kind of screwed it up here. She's written an incredible book about being unpopular which will be popular. That's just amazing. I love brands that take a stand, that have passion and aren't afraid to turn some people away. Erika has written *the* guide on how to do just that. The power of passion and community is one to be reckoned with but few understand. Take my word—this is the book that gets it."

—Scott Stratten, Unpopular Author of *UnMarketing: Stop Marketing. Start Engaging*

"The dreaded 'unpopular.' Why the hell do we accord it all manner of awfulness? Who ever convinced us that popular = good, unpopular = bad, majority rules, end of story anyhow? In business or in your personal life, it's finding *your* right people that matters. That's inbound marketing at its best. Figure out whom you serve and what you do for them and paltry issues like competition basically disappear! *When you're unpopular with all of the right people—the ones who don't want, need or understand what you have to offer—the ones who fall in love with you will eventually show up at your door.* In her hilarious, witty, read-out-loud-to-your-friends prose, Erika is that idyllic best friend you can rely on to slap you back into a reality that 'they' never told you about."

—Laura @Pistachio Fitton, Inbound Marketing Evangelist, HubSpot and coauthor, *Twitter for Dummies*

"Erika has written *the* no-nonsense, reality-driven and must-read book for anyone dreaming of starting their own business. Her writing is infectiously fun and her advice must be taken to heart by those who wish to succeed. You'll laugh, cheer and be inspired!"

—C.C. Chapman, Founder of Digital Dads and coauthor, *Content Rules: How to Create Killer Blogs, Podcasts, Videos, Ebooks, Webinars (and More) That Engage Customers and Ignite Your Business*

"Erika Napoletano has one of the most distinct and unique voices in business writing and this book reinforces those qualities from page one. And the fact that she is an entrepreneur grounds her stories and makes them not only engaging, but real. I mean, she walked away from six figures, said goodbye to her bosshole and set out on her own. At its core, that's what this book is about—taking risks, being bold, embracing failure, and snuggling up to the notion of being unpopular. A spirited and intelligent book that should make every business person dedicated to rethinking 'unpopular.'"

—Amy Cosper, Vice President and Editor-in-Chief,
Entrepreneur Magazine

"This is the first business book in a long time that grabbed me by the throat and pulled me into it. I couldn't stop reading it because it spoke to me . . . no, it sang to me! Erika Napoletano is clever though. She wrote a book here that you think is about being proud to be unpopular, but is really more about being someone who always matters to the right people, not someone who sometimes matters to just anyone. In a world that is not an end sum game, this book helps make you a winner."

—Jason Falls, Author of *No Bullshit Social Media:
The All-Business, No Hype Guide To Social Media Marketing*
and CEO of Social Media Explorer

"I've got two rules for effective marketing: (1) Try to please everyone, and you please no one. (2) The natural corollary of the first rule, which is if no one hates you, you're doing it wrong. With *The Power of Unpopular*, Erika Napoletano gives you a modern field guide to building a rabidly passionate group of fans, not just customer, clients, or prospects. Beyond knowing her stuff, Erika practices what she preaches better than just about anyone out there, which is why we all need this book within arm's reach at all times."

—Brian Clark, CEO,
Copyblogger Media

"A brilliant concept, powerfully delivered. I've already ordered six copies for my closest friends."

—Seth Godin, Author of
We Are All Weird

"If anyone understands the power of Personality: Unleashed, it's Erika. But where most people mistake snark for grit and substance, Erika actually understands core elements of a strong, irreverent brand, and makes a compelling business case for being unapologetic about who you are (because that's what your audience *really* wants from you). It's about damn time that someone did."

—Amber Naslund, Former Vice President of Strategy,
Radian6 and coauthor of *The Now Revolution*

THE **POWER** OF **UN- POPULAR**

A GUIDE TO BUILDING YOUR BRAND FOR THE AUDIENCE WHO WILL LOVE YOU (AND WHY NO ONE ELSE MATTERS)

ERIKA NAPOLETANO

WILEY

John Wiley & Sons, Inc.

Published by John Wiley & Sons, Inc., Hoboken, New Jersey.
Published simultaneously in Canada.

For general information on our other products and services or for technical support, please contact our Customer Care Department within the United States at (800) 762-2974, outside the United States at (317) 572-3993 or fax (317) 572-4002.

Wiley publishes in a variety of print and electronic formats and by print-on-demand. Some material included with standard print versions of this book may not be included in e-books or in print-on-demand. If this book refers to media such as a CD or DVD that is not included in the version you purchased, you may download this material at http://booksupport.wiley.com. For more information about Wiley products, visit www.wiley.com.

Library of Congress Cataloging-in-Publication Data:
Napoletano, Erika, 1972-
    The power of unpopular : a guide to building your brand for the audience who will love you (and why no one else matters) / Erika Napoletano.
      pages cm
    ISBN 978-1-118-13466-5 (hardback); ISBN 978-1-118-22522-6 (ebk);
ISBN 978-1-118-23866-0 (ebk); ISBN 978-1-118-26332-7 (ebk)
  1. Target marketing. 2. Branding (Marketing) 3. Target marketing–Case studies.
  4. Branding (Marketing)–Case studies.   I. Title.
    HF5415.127.N37 2012
    658.8'27–dc23   2011045220

Printed in the United States of America

10 9 8 7 6 5 4 3 2 1

For every entrepreneur who's ever wanted to let a freak flag fly.

And for my parents—who not only always let me fly mine but who also took me shopping for fabric so I could make my own.

CONTENTS

ACKNOWLEDGMENTS

There are countless people who not only contributed to my ability to be somewhat of an authority on the concept of "unpopular" but also facilitated it landing on the pages in front of you.

My parents, for instilling in me that *owning* things is a fringe benefit that stems from *doing* things and for encouraging me to become a doer. And for never offering blind support—you taught me to ask questions, gave me the tools to ask better ones, and helped me discover that having an opinion isn't poison.

Jason Schippers, for helping me own my ink and for being the first person to ever review the proposal for this book (and having done so, not telling me to burn it). You are missed.

Shelly Kramer, who made the initial introduction to John Wiley & Sons, for her mentorship and tireless interest in helping me kick ass as a business owner and brand.

Stephany Evans, my literary agent and second set of editorial eyes, for her meticulous and enthusiastic work on my behalf (and conspicuous lack of bullshit).

Merredith Branscombe, my friend, publicist, and oftentimes colleague, who is never afraid to tell me when I fuck up or call me on my crap. Two words for you: happy fish.

Darren Mahuron, my wildly talented photographer. Your mad skills with a lens combined with your friendship are a treasured asset.

My editors, Amelia and Dave, for catching the crap before you had to read it.

The Tattered Cover Bookstore in Denver, where I hammered out countless chapters and took refuge in the stacks when I had writer's block.

All of the book's contributors, a huge thanks for letting me inside your businesses and sharing your respective pieces of the deliciously unpopular pie.

The businesses featured as case studies, for not building your businesses to the lowest common denominator and creating something that made me excited to learn more. You left me inspired, and I can only hope my words did justice to what you've built and continue to refine.

All the people who told me I was too fat/mouthy/old/loud/ crass/unpopular . . . you were entirely right. Thanks for helping me find my audience . . . because *it sure ain't you.*

To you, my readers. This includes fans of Redhead Writing, readers of my *Entrepreneur Magazine* column, all of the sites who have given me a guest voice, and those who have downloaded, picked up, or checked out this book. You're the reason I get to do what I love for a living, and I'll never, ever forget that.

INTRODUCTION:
LESSONS LEARNED FROM A LIPPY
LADY ON AN AIRPLANE

In September 2011, I boarded a cross-country flight bound for Miami—I had a speaking engagement. Excited about going to Florida for the first time in several years, I settled into my window seat, grabbed a magazine, and quickly found myself joined by a woman in her 50s or 60s; her husband took the aisle while she sat in the middle. They were, to say the least, a chatty couple. Once approved electronic devices were okayed, I popped open my laptop and got to work on the finishing touches for the following day's presentation.

"Well," middle-seat lady said, "that's some salty language you have there."

She was referring to a slide that was taking up my whole screen that said, "I fucking hate PowerPoint." Let's not talk about the fact that she was reading over my shoulder.

I simply responded yes, it was—that I have a brand that allows me a certain latitude with language. Since 2007, I'd built a pretty decent following dishing out straightforward thoughts on business and life through a blog and, more recently, a column in *Entrepreneur Magazine*. I'm known for being what some might consider blue and others plainspoken, hence the words she was reading on my screen. After some not-long-enough gaps in conversation where I was able to go back to working on my presentation, she says:

"I notice that you're single."

"Umm . . . yes," I reply. "I am." *Smile.* (My left hand is devoid of adornment.)

Then, gesturing to my left arm (which was facing her), she followed with, "Well, I imagine *that* kind of limits the dating pool for you a bit," wagging her finger in and up-and-down fashion along with a squint in her eyes that said she didn't want to get too close to it.

"It" was the three-quarter-sleeve tattoo on my left arm.

I simply replied with the best response I could conjure at 36,000 feet:

"Only to those men I'd be interested in dating in the first place." *Smile*.

She then offered something to the effect of, "But of course! Oh, I didn't mean . . . [insert assorted lameness here]" and promptly went back to her Sudoku book and badgering her husband about the volume on his headset.

And That's Why We're Here

If you picked up this book in hopes of finding some *Kumbayah-flavored* business hug, you'll be disappointed. Starting, running, owning, and building a business is a path filled with an inordinate amount of bullshit, and you're signing up for many a sleepless night. My seatmate on the plane had it spot-on, annoying and abrasive though she may have been. I don't want to do business with everyone, whether in the personal or professional sense. I am unpopular (which she made quite clear). And that's something I'm going to take to the damned bank.

There's plenty of crap you can download online that will shove *Kumbayah* down your throat, prices ranging from free to *oh-my-god-it's-how-much?* You might even find it on the shelf relatively close to where you picked up this book or clicked to download it to your e-reader. I'm about unpopular thoughts and blunt advice—it's how I've built my business and brand, and this book is where they're delivered. So if you're exhausted with overnight success stories and looking for some practical insights designed to help you:

- Figure out who you are.
- Know what you bring to the table.
- Understand why you're different.
- Determine why the hell people should care about any of those things.

Read on.

I left all the crap out of this book so the editors wouldn't have to cut it out and you wouldn't be pissed about buying a book filled with crap. I'm going to have my critics about the way I share my thoughts, but hey—that's what makes me ME. The best I can ever do for you if you think that owning and running a business is what you want to do with your life is help *you* embrace *you* and leverage that single, kick-ass asset into something that will:

- Make you smile when times suck.
- Laugh hysterically when business is great.
- Make you nimble enough to shift your business in the direction that you need to at any given time in your career.

Businesses and brands begin with the people behind them. They're not logos or flashy websites, and a Twitter account or Facebook page won't thrust you into success beyond compare. If you're wondering if the path of entrepreneurship is for you, go grab a copy of Carol Roth's *The Entrepreneur Equation*. Some people are better suited to days with greater structure, being a salaried employee, and part of a more corporate team environment—and there's nothing wrong with that. It's just a metric ton different than choosing to be an entrepreneur and building a brand from the ground up (or tearing an existing one apart and rebuilding it for the better). If you've decided that you can't think of anything you'd rather do with your days than deal with the B.S. inherent in business ownership and brand building, buckle up your shit and let's get to work.

WHAT'S THE DEAL WITH UNPOPULAR? IS IT THE NEW POPULAR?

No, it's not the new popular. Popular is what we're leaving behind because, to be quite honest, it's not a tool you even need in your toolbox. It's not even a tool at all.

Every brand that's perceived as popular in the marketplace is *un*popular with a very specific demographic. Don't believe me? Take a poll and listen to the responses. Ask a group of people how they feel about Coca-Cola and Pepsi. Apple versus Microsoft. The New York

Yankees and the Boston Red Sox. The emotional responses we apply to the things we love and hate are astonishing and hold immense power for anyone looking to build a business. But before you can tap into it, you have to recognize that being *perceived* as popular and being *truly* unpopular (with just the right people) are two different things.

Being unpopular isn't the thing of nightmares. It's about:

- Embracing ideas that other people find scary and taking calculated risks.
- Honoring your target audience and learning to listen (because popular folk are too busy listening to the sound of their own voices to think that anyone else has something useful to add to the conversation).
- Having the one thing that the brands you wish you could be like understand, live by, and exude with every fiber: fiercely loyal and vocal advocates.

So although it might seem like a scary concept—building something designed to be unpopular—it's one loaded with powerful tools to help you build businesses and brands that will answer the following question each and every day:

"Have I used my passion to build something that my audience loves and can't wait to share, that grows more by the day, and earns me a living?"

SOME TIPS FOR NAVIGATING THE BOOK

The way I've structured the chapters in this book is as follows:

- **Introductory section:** A taste—consider it your cheat sheet for what follows.
- **Meat:** Things to chew on—what you need to know and why it matters.
- **Case in Point:** Most chapters will include a case study from businesses just like the one you want to build or are building to offer real-world examples of this book's principles in practice.

There aren't any "workbook" pages in this book because whenever I see those in a business book, they annoy me. I don't want to annoy you. The chapters are structured to give you actionable tasks and resources that will help you get things done. If you really need a workbook, you can rip out a few pages and grab some tape. Make your own and have a craft day.

But there is something I did instead.

When you visit the website for this book (www.unpopularbook .com), you'll find a tab called Get Into It. This will take you directly to discussion forums for each of the six "task chapters" (Chapters 2 through 7). They're interactive forums where you can discuss the book's concepts with other entrepreneurs like yourself—and me as well. I think that's a shitload more useful than a workbook. You can learn more about accessing these online resources in Appendix B.

As I mentioned, most of the book's chapters include a case study from a brand or company similar to the one you're aspiring to build or are in the midst of building. Chances are, you've never heard of most of these brands, and that's for one simple reason: you weren't supposed to. These business owners have built their brands so well that they command their space, and maybe theirs isn't one you play in, which is okay. But instead of the case studies we read all too often from behemoth brands like Zappos, Southwest Airlines, and Disney, it might be just a hair easier to emulate what's worked for the businesses featured in the chapters that follow. Read, learn, do—and I want to get you from reading to doing (and doing things that work) in the shortest time possible.

So, let's do it. As already mentioned, building a brand—especially an unpopular one—is a *metric ton* of work. If you're game, however, we can make that work pay off and create a business and brand you'll love that's true to both you and your audience with the potential to generate enough revenue that you can work on creating more. And if it fails (and some businesses do), the goal is to fail fast and move on to the next venture, wiser than you were before.

THE **POWER** OF **UN-POPULAR**

CHAPTER 1

RETHINKING UNPOPULAR

Back in high school, my friends and I weren't going to win any popularity contests, but we were the ones who all the popular kids crowded around on test days so they could copy off our papers. We were never cheerleaders or star athletes, but we won more accolades for the school than the sports teams did. We went to high school dances as a group, and all of the social glory that went with those formative years—well, we missed it. We knew what unpopular was. It was the opposite of cool. Maybe we were cool among our friends, but we weren't the ones with crowns and tiaras on prom night.

And today, nobody gives a damn.

IT'S TIME TO LEAVE THE PLAYGROUND, DONTCHA THINK?

Who gives a rat's ass who was picked first or last at kickball or who walked away with a plastic tiara or crown on prom night? Today, we look back at those days with a bit of disdain, because most of us have become wise enough to realize something so simple: **popularity isn't important.** And as smart businesspeople, popular is the last thing we ever want to become.

That's not a message you can deliver on playgrounds or in high school gymnasiums, but popular is the last thing smart businesspeople should ever want to become. And there's nothing at all wrong with having achieved popularity with the people who surrounded you in your formative years. When it can cause problems is when we rely on it in business, because it's pretty damn useless.

Let's go with the World English Dictionary's definition of *popular:* "appealing to the general public; widely favored or admired."

If you're looking to build a business (or life) that makes you appealing to the general public, I'll go ahead and say that you're poised for a life of disappointment. Just think about the most important people in your life—their quirks, nuances, and talents. You have them in your life because, for all they are (including each of those equally fabulous and maddening qualities), they suit you and *make your life better.* It's the quirks, nuances, and talents you remember, not the plain vanilla things they do. The general public? That's plain vanilla.

And that's why people and businesses that find success in this life, in any regard, have changed their opinion of what being unpopular really means. They've left the general public behind, knowing that reaching them is a futile endeavor; and instead, they have set their sights on a specific audience.

The builders of unpopular brands are looking to make new inroads. They take the current standards, break them apart, and re-shape them into something that fits people who have been left behind or left wanting more. The last thing they're striving for is to be is liked by the general public, because they understand that not even Walmart has something for everyone. And being unpopular can be a scary thing, because we all know how people hate change and we don't know that people will like our particular flavor of unpopular. Some won't. But some will, and that's the audience that matters. Pretty contrary to those playground politics and the "Did you bring enough for the rest of the class?" mentality we were raised with, isn't it? That's why we're leaving the playground and deciding to do business instead.

BY THE WAY . . . WHO THE HELL AM I?

I'm the unpopular girl.

And all that crap I put up with in school? Priceless. In fact, being that geeky, unpopular kid caused me to learn some pretty wicked lessons. I came to understand that if something was going to work, it was up to me to make it happen. I also knew that the trendiest blue jeans and hippest sneakers weren't going to get me a job. I started to realize that, to me at least, the coolest people in the world were people who made things happen. People who changed things and made people think differently. People who, without any fanfare, were de-signed to survive—and thrive.

All through history, it has been the same way.

Thomas Edison had only three months of formal schooling but turned out to be one of the most prolific inventors in U.S. history, holding 1,093 patents in his name. (He was also afraid of the dark.)

After being awarded his secondary degree in 1900, Albert Einstein searched two years for a teaching job to no avail; in 1921, he was awarded the Nobel Prize in Physics.

It was more than money, academic achievement, or social standing that made these people *do* extraordinary things. It was something *inside* them. For 17 years, I tried to do things everyone else's way and be one of the "supposed tos": you're supposed to get a job, get promoted, make more money, buy a nicer car, get married, and save for retirement.

And none of that worked for me.

What I wanted to do was do wasn't a popular idea with anyone in my life—I wanted to take a risk and pursue what I loved, which was writing and figuring out solutions to problems. So one day in early 2007, I made the really unpopular decision to leave my six-figure gig and went to work as a junior copywriter for a boutique advertising agency in Las Vegas, Nevada.

I'd never been happier in my life.

About the same time, I started blogging and got thrown into social media in true baptism-by-fire fashion as one of my roles at the new agency. Bit by bit, I was finding new readers, starting new conversations, and discovering what I loved—marketing, branding, and helping people understand where they fit. As someone who was just finding where *she* fit, I was on the same journey.

That led me to Denver, Colorado, having left the ad agency and taken on a real estate technology start-up as my main client, along with becoming an investor. I outsourced all the freelance work I'd accumulated, as this was my first real opportunity to live my dream, going full monty in writing, marketing, and problem solving—and it jazzed me every day for nine months. We were bootstrapped, all of us giving what we could (and beyond), and there came a day where I realized (or rather, my bank account did) that I hadn't drawn a paycheck in over two months.

I walked into the conference room and asked the chief executive officer (CEO) and chief financial officer (CFO) when they thought I'd be able to take a draw, as things were getting tight.

That's when they told me the company was out of money.

That was a Thursday. The following Monday, I woke up with nowhere to go. I'd given something a shot, it failed, and there I was with the next decision needing to be made. Aside from walking out of that six-figure gig over a year prior, this was the best thing to have happened to me yet.

MY "TODAY" AS AN ENTREPRENEUR

I was a super shitty W2 employee, and it was clear long before I admitted it that I wasn't meant to work according to someone else's rules. With no other choices than to sink or swim, I got off the couch and set about figuring out my assets.

Money? (Cue unbridled, mocking laughter.)

Over 17 years of sales and marketing skills? Check.

A small, but growing audience surrounding my blog and social media activities? Check.

Some talent with words? Apparently.

I fully owned the knowledge that I wasn't for everyone, but I was bound and determined to find more of the people who appreciated what I was doing online through my two blogs and social media accounts. I pulled back in that freelance work I'd outsourced, cultivated relationships, and kept doing what I was doing, learning something every step along the way. From September 2009 (which was the On the Couch date) to early 2011, I'd built an even bigger audience—and it was one that participated, one that shared with me as much as I shared with them. I guess people noticed. My brand had become this go-to source for an irreverent, in-your-face perspective on business, marketing, and life in general and that happened only for three reasons: the audience, their willingness to share what I was doing, and my commitment to own everything about my brand. In early 2011, I was invited to write a regular monthly column for *Entrepreneur Magazine* and was then offered the opportunity to write this book.

But . . .

I'VE NEVER HEARD OF YOU. WHY SHOULD I LISTEN TO ANYTHING YOU HAVE TO SAY?

Fair question, and one I even asked myself! When I was approached to write this book, all I could think was, "Who the hell am I to tell this story?" In the middle of one of my laments, a friend of mine stopped me by smacking her hand down on the table and said quite plainly, "You're just like everyone else who's taken a risk and started something. The only difference is you're not on the front page of magazines."

She was right.

I'm just like you. And I think that maybe people were tired of getting business advice from people who *aren't* just like them. Whether we aspire to make headlines or simply be a household name in our own neck of the woods, I know we all share two common goals: to be great businesspeople and to build brands that become integral parts of the communities in which we live and industries in which we excel.

So, what a person like me can do for a person like you is show you the power I see each and every day in being unpopular and how you can use that power to differentiate yourself in a meaningful way from those who believe that the line in the middle of the road is the best place to open a business. And it all begins with giving failure a big, fat hug.

FAILURE: A *SUPER* UNPOPULAR CONCEPT

It's the looming question: What if my business venture fails? Well, it's highly likely. (I know—I'm such a killjoy.) More than 700,000 new businesses are launched in the United States alone each year (see Figure 1.1). Of those, only two-thirds survive the first two years and less than half make it to the four-year point (statistics courtesy of the

Figure 1.1
Kauffman Foundation Chart

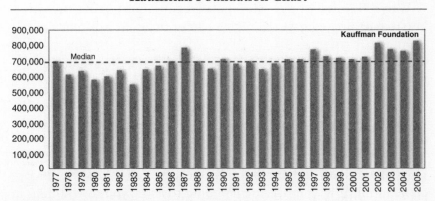

Source: "Exploring Firm Formation: Why Is the Number of New Firms Constant?" The Kaufmann Foundation, 2010.

Small Business Administration). Somewhere along your entrepreneurial path, you're going to start a business or have an idea that ultimately fails—just like you're going to do things in your personal life that don't work out so great every now and then. So here's my question: When did we start holding our businesses to standards of success that we can't even maintain as human beings?

Talk about needing to cut ourselves some slack! Failure is a rite of passage. We should learn to fail fast and often, yet differently each time. When we do, we can quickly get through the shit that doesn't work and find the things that do, which lets us get on with the business of creating something great. In the same way that a breakup doesn't mean we'll never find a companion again, having a business venture fail doesn't preclude you going on to building something that's everything you wanted in a business.

So how does this apply to businesses designed to be popular and those who embrace the power of unpopular?

If you build a business in order to be popular, you're going to fail—and fail the same way every time.

Why? Because you take the same path, and it's the path of following someone or something else. It's devoid of innovation and instead uses "me too" concepts that don't give anyone a reason to care about what you're doing or why.

If you build a business designed to be unpopular with just the right audience, although you might fail, too, you're going to fail *differently* each time.

Why? Because you're thinking, creating, and being proactive. You're pursuing your vision with a pair of titanium balls and a gleam in your eye.

One model is destined for failure. One has a chance at success. Which one do you want to have a go at?

FAILURE? INEVITABLE. UNPOPULAR? POWERFUL!

Hug failure. Roll up next to it in bed every night and spoon it. Become intimate with it because it's going to allow you to do things in life and business that those who are afraid to fail can only imagine. Entrepreneurs use great relationships and great ideas to give things a go with both feet in the pool, and they understand that being unpopular isn't about changing what they do and who they are for the people who aren't their fans . . . it's about finding the people who will love them.

Acknowledging that your brand is unpopular isn't about being disliked—it's about knowing who will best be served by what you want to build. Just think about the possibilities for your business when you:

- Stop focusing on pleasing the people who are never going to like you, your product, your service.
- Learn more about the ones who already do (and just don't know it).
- Can focus 100 percent of your efforts on building a business for *that* audience instead of spinning your wheels on the myth of universal popularity.

Harry Potter—The Ultimate Unpopular Brand

Although she might be the stuff dreams are made of to aspiring writers and people who like wizardry, J. K. Rowling's life prior to Harry's rise to Hogwarts-flavored success was anything but a dream. Living on government assistance as a single mother whose own mother had recently passed away, Rowling's first incarnation of the Harry Potter series took her years to complete and was rejected by 12 publishing houses. She finally received an offer on the first manuscript in 1996, along with a whopping advance of £1,500, or roughly $2,250 in those days. Try to tell a single mother not to spend all of that in one place.

Flash forward to today. The last four books in the Harry Potter series all consecutively set records as the fastest-selling books in history, and the brand itself is estimated to be worth in excess of $15 billion (figure as of 2007).

It's not popular to follow your gut. In fact it's anything but in most cases. Truth be told, I'd never picked up a Harry Potter book until 2011 out of sheer spite for the worldwide phenomenon. I was damned if I was going to hop on the Hogwarts Express. But sometimes, you keep hearing about things because they truly are so exceptional that people can't stand to *not* talk about them, which is why I turned my first page of Harry Potter (finally) in 2011.

This is the kind of brand and reputation we as entrepreneurs should strive to build—unpopular with all of the people who will never love you or will be the tough sell and pure nectar to those who will admire, follow, and, most important, share what you love to do with everyone they know. It doesn't matter what the current size of your business is or what its eventual scale will be; brand advocacy is brand advocacy. The power of unpopular rests in understanding those who will love what you do and the persistence involved in finding them. Just as Harry Potter wasn't an out-of-the-gate hit, great brands take time to develop traction, and it's a continual process of evaluating your audience and refining your message so that you keep the eyes you want on you, unconcerned if others look away.

Sure, there are people out there who hate the Harry Potter books for some reason (or like me, for no reason at all). What you build will have the same critics—justified or not.

So we've figured out that being unpopular isn't about being disliked and that, yeah, there will people along the way who will hate what we build (and some for no good reason). What will people think about you if you decide to build an unpopular brand?

DOES BEING UNPOPULAR MEAN I'M AN ASSHOLE (OR HAVE TO BECOME ONE)?

No. In fact, the people who build unpopular brands are just the opposite and understand that it's not about seeking to offend, tearing other people down, or yelling the loudest. Pick up a copy of Robert Sutton's *The No Asshole Rule* if you're in doubt. Unpopular business strategies offer no harbor for asshole behavior and if you're offended by that vernacular, take it up with Sutton—he's a professor at Stanford and I'll defer to his expert grasp on both the word and concept. I think that we'd all do better by taking an anti-asshole approach to the Path to Unpopular and embrace the following from the start:

- **Humility:** It's impossible to get everything done on one's own, and the sooner you acknowledge that you need a team to get you from point A to point Z and every point in between, the better off you'll be. Ask for help, know what you don't know, say thank you often, and never be afraid to admit it when you're wrong. (Four rather unpopular acts for people who are supposed to be self-sufficient, no?)

- **Including While Excluding:** Building great companies and brands (and consequently, human beings) isn't merely about being exclusive. The more you seek to include the people who are influenced by your business decisions, the more clearly you can get a sense for how we can better serve the people we wish to please. In the tech-laden, referral-based business culture that rules the lives of many, consumers flock not only to brands where they have a voice but to brands that they feel truly *hear* them. It's important to remember, however, that every brand excludes someone by nature—and that's part of what we're going to figure out.

- **Purpose:** It's the *why* behind your motivations and what guides you. Although these motivations can change over time, understanding the purpose that drives your business decisions at any given time is imperative. Unpopular brands stick to their guns (even when sticking to your guns sucks) because they know doing so is for the best over the long haul. There also comes a time where there may be disagreements about your brand's purpose and direction, and those times make for great conversations because purpose is something that can't be a divided issue. (We'll discuss this more in Chapter 7.)

BUT HOW DOES BEING UNPOPULAR HELP ME BUILD A BETTER BUSINESS?

Although being unpopular might never have scored you a date to the prom or a featured position in the yearbook, becoming comfortable with unpopular holds an inherent power your competitors aren't willing to tap. By taking the three anti-asshole principles just discussed, we can begin to look at how following the path toward unpopular enables us to be better at them, and in turn build better businesses:

- **Unpopular thinkers hate sheep:** Not of the barnyard variety, but of the shortsighted-thinking variety. You innovate, create, and break down the norms because you see better solutions and underserved audiences yearning to be noticed. You seek out unconventional solutions to conventional problems because you've never been wrapped in the protective, chocolate-flavored outer coating of popular thought that keeps us from coming up with our own ideas. You are the ones who notice.

- **Unpopular brands love critics:** Remember when we were told to embrace constructive criticism? Being unpopular holds the power of making your critics work in your favor. This is so epic that I had no choice but to give the subject its own chapter. (Try to resist the urge to flip forward to Chapter 8, okay?) Critics make us better. Assholes don't. You—the unpopular thinker—know the difference.

- **Unpopular brands don't have a backup plan:** If you're afraid to make a jump, that fear goes into every decision you make. This is why we talked about getting on touchy-feely terms with failure. Commitment can't be faked, and unpopular brands need it by the bucketload. Unpopular thinkers work without a net and invest everything you have into what you love—because that's how shit gets done.

Unpopular strategies are more powerful than the *popular* crap we've been fed for eons. They'll do more to help you build better businesses and create fiercely loyal audiences than any tactic you can pull out of an MBA program. So how do we get from where we are to unpopular? Let's head to the kitchen before we launch some half-baked idea. We need a recipe.

A RECIPE FOR UNPOPULARITY: FIVE INGREDIENTS

When I sat down and looked at every brand I'd encountered in the marketplace that had found any level of longevity and success, they each demonstrated an understanding and daily practice of these five elements. From my favorite local restaurant here in Denver to the larger-than-life brands that decorate pop culture, it didn't matter the size or scale. It just matters that they understand *all* of these qualities and don't just go through the motions—they weave them seamlessly into their business cultures.

- **Personality:** Your brand is a who and never a what. People do business with people.
- **Approachability:** If you haven't created a personality that lets your audience know they can talk to your brand, you need to rethink the personality you created.
- **Sharability:** Your brand personality along with the welcome mat you put out for your audience dictates how, why, and how often people share you with the people in their lives (also known as your potential customers).
- **Scalability:** Every unpopular brand pays attention to infrastructure—if you've spent the effort on creating an approachable personality that makes your audience want to share your brand, growth is inevitable and you must be able to deal with it.
- **Profitability:** You've invested in the who and put out the welcome mat. Word's gotten around, and you're growing. You've built the infrastructure to support the growth. Now, how do you make sure you remain solvent and keep on track so that you can point your brand toward generating revenue? The emotional and practical implications of profitability.

For the remainder of this book, these are the five ingredients we'll be working with in our big ol' business-building kitchen. But this whole "unpopular" thing . . .

WILL IT WORK?

The only determining factors in whether anything you set out to accomplish will find success are you, the market, and a shitload of perseverance. What you'll get here are some tools to use as you get into the thick of things and show you, step by step, how to establish a foundation for your business that can:

- Withstand changes in the economic climate.
- Tune out the assholes and tune in to your audience.
- Start becoming something that the audience you seek to serve will appreciate, share, and continue to patronize.
- Put a smile on your face more days than not because you're doing something you love for a living—no matter how big you

become, how many people work for you, or whether or not you find yourself in the headlines.

And I didn't mention a thing about making money.

The pages that follow will have few references to money and none to the speed at which you can expect to start stashing some away in the bank. Even Chapter 7—where we discuss profitability—is less a chapter about making gobs of money than one on building your business so that you don't wake up one day and realize you've been working for free. Making money from a business is a by-product of doing good business—and every unpopular brand is built to do just that.

In addition to being a literary icon, Henry David Thoreau was also a pragmatic man who offered entrepreneurial spirits a tip on how to perceive wealth acquired along life's road: "A man is rich in proportion to the number of things he can afford to let alone."

This is why I run a business—so that I might have the means to let some things alone. It's also a part of every unpopular business, deciding what you can (and should) let alone or let others take responsibility for. *That* is how we all can buy time and spend it on the things we hold dear. So although you can't spend money to buy time, you can build a business that will make both for you.

So yes, the "unpopular" things works, and the next step is actually building that unpopular business (which I know you're chomping at the bit to do). But first let's take a trip to Kidron, Ohio, so that I can introduce you to J. E. Lehman, a guy whose parents told him he should probably figure out what he wanted to do for a living. And boy—did he!

CASE IN POINT: THE STORY OF LEHMAN'S

BY NO ONE'S RULES

Kidron, Ohio, is a small town whose current-day population tips the scales around 600 residents. You'd never guess that it's home to a 42,000-square-foot hardware store that sprawls between four pre–Civil War–era buildings and welcomes between 500,000 and 750,000 people through its doors each year.

They sell more oil lamps than electric ones.

You're more likely to find a wide selection of butter churns than 17 different interior paints in butter yellow.

They are the primary supplier of period-specific, nonelectrical appliances to Hollywood productions.

And it all started because J. E. (or Junior, as he was called back then) Lehman's parents asked him just *what* he was going to do for a living.

The History

Kidron was founded in the early 1800s by Swiss Mennonites seeking religious freedom in the Americas. The surrounding area welcomed others of a similar religious and farming ilk, including the Amish. Just like every small town in any country, there was a little hardware store that opened in Kidron in 1915. It sold everything from heating oil to Dodge automobiles; a population of a few hundred whose faith was about self-reliance didn't need more than one store to supply what they couldn't build at home. But this store wasn't Lehman's.

In 1955, J. E. Lehman returned home to Kidron from volunteering service overseas for the Mennonite missionary community. Soon after his arrival, J. E. knew the farming lifestyle wasn't one that suited him, so his parents put it on the line: if you're not going to be a farmer, what are you going to do for a living? After a long discussion, J. E. decided he wanted to buy the town's hardware store. His father approved of the move and lent him the money to make the purchase. And *that's* when Lehman's came to Kidron, Ohio.

Jay Lehman had always admired the simplistic way of life the growing Amish population brought to his part of the Ohio valley. They were a steadfast farming culture steeped in values and

(continued)

(*continued*)

eschewed the newfangled technologies (like electricity) that were cropping up left and right after World War II. He thought it'd be a shame if future generations were unable to enjoy the benefits that his community enjoyed, created by the do-it-yourself nature of the Amish culture, so they became his target customer—he was going to do everything he could with his new little hardware store to ensure they had what they needed.

Even with his enthusiastic approach to the store, business was rather slow during the first months. So slow, in fact, that he had to hire his father—the one who lent him the money to buy the store in the first place—to watch the store each day so that he could drive a school bus to earn enough money to pay back his father's loan. So here was Jay Lehman—outstanding loan to his father, working a second job to pay him back, hiring him to watch the store so that he could go earn more money, and choosing to cater to a population that shunned modern conveniences. Probably not a course a career counselor would advise one to take, and certainly not one that followed what many would consider popular conventions for building a business.

The hardware store chugged along. In the early 1960s, Jay Lehman hired people to run the store while he went off on a two-year assignment with the missionary community to open a travel agency in Africa. Two years turned into four . . . six . . . and eventually more than ten. In his overseas adventures he came across the same situation repeatedly: people in the world who had unreliable sources of electricity, if any sources at all. (Do you see where this is headed?)

Two Things: Luck and Timing

In the early 1970s, Jay Lehman returned from his missionary trip and came back to his hardware store. "A good business is the beneficiary of two things," he states: "Luck and timing." The year 1973 brought both to his doorstep.

When Lehman went to place an order for some wood-burning cooking stoves with one of the manufacturers he frequently patronized, he learned they were no longer going to be carrying the model he wanted. Knowing that his target audience—the local Amish community—relied heavily on these stoves for their day-to-day needs, he asked what he had to do to keep them in stock. The answer? He could buy a three-year supply.

What would be completely absurd to any sane businessperson, Jay Lehman did without a second thought: he took out a second mortgage on his house and bought a three-year supply of wood-burning stoves.

Right about this time, OPEC initiated an oil embargo primarily targeted at the United States and oil skyrocketed from $3 per barrel to nearly $12. Gasoline and heating oil came at a premium, and natural gas wasn't the prevalent resource it is today.

Jay Lehman's three-year supply of wood-burning stoves sold out in six months. Luck and timing—he had them in spades. But no entrepreneur is content with slam-bam success, and Lehman was already working on what was next. All those profits from the stoves went right back into the business. The town of Kidron was starting to see customers coming from as far away as Pennsylvania, all of them in search of the anachronistic nonelectrical appliances that comprised the bulk of Lehman's inventory.

Flash Forward

A lot's happened at Lehman's since the 1973 energy crisis. They launched a catalog not long after and became one of the pioneers of the mail-order age, a move that exploded sales across the country. And remember Jay's missionary stints during World War II and then following in Africa? Well, that information he'd gathered about all of those places that had unreliable or no electricity sure did come back around to help his business. His missionary connections who still served those areas

(*continued*)

(*continued*)

went to Jay's store for everything they needed that couldn't be acquired locally.

When the late 1980s and early 1990s rolled around, Jay's son Galen heard about these invisible connections that were going to help people across the globe communicate. Naturally, he was talking about the Internet, and (thankfully) Galen has the same entrepreneurial spirit as his father. When most people were skeptical about "this Internet," Lehman's was already selling product online (a Mennonite-owned business catering to the Amish community built a website?). To this day, Lehman's website remains a resource not only for their domestic customers but also for the loyal customers around the world who discovered the little hardware store in Ohio only through those "invisible connections." What began as a skeptical and wary network of information became the way for many global consumers to acquire hard-to-find tools and appliances not available anywhere else.

Enter Y2K

Remember the OPEC embargo? The entire Y2K scare of 1998 and 1999 proved to be another huge boost for Lehman's seemingly narrow target demographic. Mainstream America started to discover this store that carried products and tools that would prove useful when the computers stopped working when the clocks struck 2000. For the two years leading up to Y2K, the dozen phone lines leading into the store were incessantly ringing and Lehman's staff were answering more and more questions from the curious about how to do *this* and what they needed to do *that* in case of the grid going down. The buzz of activity and interest from novice customers made the Lehman team—now comprised of Jay and his son Galen and daughter Glenda—think: What if we started showing people how to use all these things we sell? Once again, they were on to something.

The looming threat of what could happen on Y2K sparked a renaissance of the do-it-yourself lifestyle and new, interested customers took to the Lehmans' guidance with fervor. Things that were once considered old suddenly had new relevance, and customers felt empowered. Y2K didn't mean anyone had to stop living when (and if) the predicted downfall happened, and on top of it all, Lehman's had found a new way to demonstrate the relevance of these "old things" to those living more modern lifestyles than his original target demographic.

When Y2K passed without fanfare, Glenda described the in-store environment as quiet. "You could throw a baseball from one end of our showroom to another and not hit a single customer." So what did Lehman's do? Again, they took the least likely path and chose to expand. "We had to ask ourselves if we'd saturated the market. Had we really reached every possible customer there was to reach? If our showroom was this quiet, we needed to do an even better job than we have with Y2K in showing people how our products fit into their lives," she said.

Today, Lehman's continues to be a destination. In their showroom, customers and visitors can find everything from butter-churning demonstrations to a $5,000 hand-hammered copper bathtub to an actual Boneshaker-style bicycle that tips the scales around $800. The store isn't just a place for people to indulge in a bit of nostalgia—it's a living testament to Jay Lehman's original business goal: preserving the simple conventions of the surrounding Amish community for generations to come. "If there's something like a butter churn on our shelves, it will churn butter. You can use it as a daffodil vase if you want, but it works. We sell things that—while they might be simple, they work," explains Glenda. Although it might be considered a buzzword, Lehman's has achieved *authenticity* in the truest sense of Webster's definition: "original, primary, first-hand, one who does things himself." Lehman's products, work ethic, and way of embracing the education of customers speaks volumes—which means

(continued)

(*continued*)

Lehman's has never found the need to scream from the rooftops about who they are and what they believe.

And if you're interested, Glenda *has* used one of their small butter churns as a daffodil vase. But she also uses it to make butter.

AN UNPOPULAR BRAND BUILT BY THE MOST UNLIKELY MAN

Now, you probably wouldn't have thought you'd pick up this book and find one of the first case studies to be one featuring a Mennonite missionary who decided to buy a hardware store that served the local Amish community.

And that's the point.

Whatever your perception of popular has been, it's time to rethink it. The smartest people among us in the business world are pioneers of unpopular ideas and understand something that the popular kids never will: building, growing, and running a business has less to do with what you have to sell than it does the size of and your connection with the audience you're committed to serve.

Jay Lehman? Committed. Did he ever think he'd be the namesake behind a 42,000-square-foot retail location supported by a 100,000-square-foot warehouse and both Hollywood's and the world's go-to source for "if you think you can't find that anymore, think again" appliances? Was his goal to be the only business from Kidron, Ohio, featured on the town's Wikipedia page? Nope. He's just a man who "likes old stuff" and wanted to do his part to preserve some really cool pieces of history for generations to come. All along the way he listened to his customers and found even more ways to show them how this "old stuff" fulfilled their modern-day needs.

When you're unpopular with all of the right people—the ones who don't want, need, or understand what you have to offer—the ones who fall in love with you will eventually show up at your door. Or in the case of Lehman's, your parking lot. Jay Lehman likes to look at the license plates in the parking lot of his store from time to time, and on Black Friday in 2010, he did just that. That day he'd counted plates from 32 different states.

Not too shabby for a country boy with an eighth-grade education who decided to open a hardware store specializing in nonelectrical appliances.

So let's get on with the business of building an unpopular business, just like J. E. Lehman did. The first step is finding the people who will love us (which sure ain't the entire class), as there's no sense in performing a Broadway play in an empty theater.

CHAPTER 2

IDENTIFYING YOUR AUDIENCE

If you've never stumbled across the name Randy Pausch before now, you've been missing out. Turn on your computer, get on over to YouTube, and enter "Randy Pausch last lecture" in the search box.[1] Then clear the next 76 minutes of your schedule, and possibly at least another 60 minutes after that to collect yourself. Without offering any spoilers, I'll share a bit of Randy's story, even though he's the only one who can truly do it justice.

Randy was an academic, a professor of computer science and one of the world's pioneer researchers and instructors in virtual reality. The father of three was diagnosed with pancreatic cancer in 2006 and set about the journey of not only facing the fact that pancreatic cancer yielded no survivors but also figuring out what he could do with the time he had left. Retiring professors at Carnegie Mellon had historically been asked to participate in what was referred to as the Last Lecture series—what would they say to their students if they knew they were going to die? Pausch did what no other professor had done previously: he delivered his last lecture under exactly that reality.

He'd devoted his life to achieving his childhood dreams, from walking in zero gravity to becoming an Imagineer for Walt Disney. And through this process of pursuing what he loved, he found that one of his greatest joys was creating an environment where others—students—could openly pursue their dreams as well. As the founder of numerous academic programs that crossed disciplines, crushed convention, and gave today's students a chance to make a difference in tomorrow's world, Randy was a man who understood identifying niches. During his address at Carnegie Mellon's commencement ceremony in 2008, he said, "The size of your audience doesn't matter. What's important is that your audience is listening."

Something leading academics like Randy Pausch understand as well as any entrepreneur is the importance of niche. They know that in order to facilitate change, you must:

---

[1] You can also go to the website for this book (www.UnpopularBook.com) and visit the Resources page. You'll find this video embedded in the section for Chapter 2.

- Identify the problem you wish to solve.
- Acknowledge that there is a need to solve the problem and that there is an audience who will appreciate your eventual solution.
- Understand that there are more than a few people who will never get what it is you do or why you bother with it.
- Present your solution to the people who will appreciate it in a way they will understand, because your solution really doesn't mean anything without their eventual adoption of it.

So watch Randy Pausch's Last Lecture or pick up the book. It's a beautiful read. The work begins with your audience, and as Randy states, it doesn't matter what size your audience is. What matters is that they're listening. So let's take a page from academia and start with the problem: you can't get your audience to listen if you don't know to whom you're talking in the first place.

We'll break this down into the four following steps:

- **Clarifying** your reason for being.
- **Understanding** who will benefit from and want what you have to offer.
- **Finding** those people, talking to them, and using them to help build your brand.
- **Knowing the importance of** your brand story—how you can use what you've learned to tell a story your customers want to hear.

Before we go into this any further, there's something we need to make perfectly clear . . .

PRODUCT IS PRODUCT IS PRODUCT

Let's deal with this now so that we can leave it alone for the rest of the book: product is product is product. Everyone who has a business sells a "widget," be it physical, intellectual, or virtual. Make sure your widget rocks. No amount of branding, unpopular or otherwise, will help you successfully sell a crappy product for very long. If you want to be around in 5, 10, or 20 years, make sure your product is actually worthwhile. Although SkyMall would have us think there's a market for anything, there's not.

Product's got to be good. Got it? Good.

Now, let's figure out why you're going to do this thing called building a business.

CLARIFYING YOUR REASON FOR BEING

For a business to have legs, its reason for being has to be more than that you were shafted for paychecks by too many start-ups or couldn't stand being a part of the nine-to-five machine. Although frustration is a killer motivator, businesses exist to solve (and continue solving) problems and you have to identify the one (or ones) you want to solve.

It's time to get our hands dirty. Grab a shovel.

WELCOME TO THE SANDBOX

Sure, we may be leaving the playground antics behind, but when you find a problem that needs solving, you're going to find other people who are already solving a related, similar, or even the same problem. Let's spend a little time talking about the "me too" economy and how unpopular brands differentiate themselves from the copycat antics that blow across the business landscape like dandelion fuzz.

We'll start with a question:

If you're going to take the time and spend the energy to develop a company and its brand, why would you waste your time doing something that other people are already doing?

NO SUCH THING AS A BUSINESS IN A BOX

Even if you look at the world of franchises—the world where you really can buy a business in a box—you'll find that the most successful franchise owners understand that acquiring the franchise license is only a small part of the success of the business. It doesn't matter if you have the strength of a nationally recognized brand like McDonald's or Massage Envy hanging over your front door. We've all been to franchise business locations that are out-standing and then gone to another in the same franchise that's completely forgettable if not horrible. It's up to *you* to create a business culture that appreciates your clients and customers and offers an experience that keeps them coming back for more.

It's completely erroneous to think that a great problem is enough if you're going to go about solving it in a completely unoriginal way. In fact, I'd go so far as to say it's insulting to your prospective customers and most of all to yourself. It's also lazy. Unpopular brands aren't lazy. They're working tirelessly, making sure that their energy is directed toward solving the right problem for the right audience and in the right way. So if you think you're going to launch a social media con-sulting business because you see other people making killing at it (or at least *saying* they're making a killing) or you're going to open a neighborhood coffee shop simply because the block with the For Lease sign doesn't have a coffee house on it and you know the one 2 miles away always has a line out the door, those are shitty reasons to jump into the sandbox. "Me too" people are followers not leaders; they're the knockoff Rolexes of the business world. They look great at first glance, but when you look harder at how long they're going to last, you're in for a shocker.

However, if you can look at either scenario—the consulting business or coffee shop—and believe you can improve on what the other play-ers are doing, the conversation starts to get interesting. Mess around with the sand, getting it into places where the sun doesn't shine, and make sure you're still dumping it out of your shoes weeks from now. There might also come a time where you see a sandbox of fellow busi-nesspeople that you want to hop into, but it seems awfully crowded. How do you figure out if it's worth trying to wedge yourself in?

IS THE SANDBOX TOO CROWDED?

There's not a day that goes by that we don't hear about a new company offering a new approach to some task or activity we've been doing for quite some time. The truth is there are few empty sandboxes for new companies to build in; most are already filled with castles—or at least very decent bungalows—built by others. But should that deter us from getting in the box and starting to dig? In a conversation I had with Jason Mendelson, cofounder and managing director of the Foundry Group (a leading venture capital firm specializing in early stage technology companies) and coauthor of *Venture Deals: Be Smarter Than Your Lawyer and Venture Capitalist,* he had this to say about the problems companies set out to solve and the decision to enter into a seemingly crowded business space:

> You can't disregard second and third mover companies. Some companies that others perceived as being late to the party really cleaned house: Facebook was after MySpace, Google was after AOL, Excite, and Yahoo! And eBay and Amazon were late to the party, too. I think there's a huge second and third mover advantage if the market isn't completely locked-up. But regardless of whether you're a first mover or seeking to improve upon companies currently offering solutions, it's true that 99 percent of people don't really understand their own "secret sauce."

Markets are moved by that secret sauce. What's yours?

FINDING YOUR SAUCE

Talk to me about Dijon mustard. In my world, there's not a single sandwich in existence that wouldn't taste better with a little dab of Dijon. For some of you, it might be hot sauce. And there are definitely some of you who wouldn't even touch a sandwich with either of these condiments on it.

Your brand's secret sauce isn't something *magical* that makes everyone like your brand. Rather, your secret sauce is something *particular* that will attract one group and possibly repel another. So what's the condiment, or secret sauce, that's going to set you apart and attract the people who love the new way you have of doing things?

People are creatures of habit who prefer to keep doing the same old things. There are people who can't fathom a cup of coffee that doesn't take six Latin derivatives and a five-dollar bill to order, while there are those who have never sipped a cup they didn't make in their own kitchen. There's no shortage of problems in the marketplace that are ripe for solutions, but how will your solutions be *different*—and *better*—than the ones currently available? A substantial part of answering that question is understanding for whom you're creating them—and, more important, for whom you're not.

UNDERSTANDING WHO REALLY WANTS WHAT YOU'VE GOT

If we take a moment and look at the colossal brands in today's culture, they all appear to have something in common: people can't stop talking about them. What people are *really* talking about is their secret sauce. Good, bad, rave reviews or total pans—*indifference* isn't a word that ever comes to mind. Although they might seem astronomically popular on the surface, there's always another side to the equation. If Oprah Winfrey had built her media empire hoping that everyone would tune in to watch her show, love her guests, follow her advice, and buy her magazine, she would have failed miserably. The people who liked who she was, what she put out there, and how she delivered her message came along for the ride. "Lots of people want to ride with you in the limo," says Oprah. "But what you want is someone who will take the bus with you when the limo breaks down." In one sentence, she's identified what you should demand of your target demographic.

Oprah didn't build her brand for people like me. (Admittedly, I'm much more an Ellen DeGeneres–type of gal.) Zappos didn't build their online shoe empire for bargain hunters. Southwest Airlines doesn't cater to the traveler who relishes assigned seating and first-class accommodations. So let's set ourselves to the same exercise as these big boys—understanding who isn't going to be a fan of who they are and what they do—and use that information to make the visions we have for who needs and loves us more clear.

LOVING THE PEOPLE WHO WILL NEVER LOVE US

The people who will never love your brand are the greatest gift you could ever receive as a businessperson. They deliver their opinions in the purest shades of black and white, and you can start using them *right now* to help clearly define your target audience.

Let's start to get a feel for what these people look like. Make a chart with two columns and label them like this (or write in this book—you paid for it):

People who will never use us:	Why:

Throw some margaritas in the blender and get to filling it in. Here are some criteria to get you started:

- Price points (luxury versus budget)
- Geography (local retailer versus online retailer)
- Sophistication of service (full service or do-it-yourself)
- Platform (iOS versus Android)

If you can get one audience in there, you can get a whole heap of them. This is the fun part—it's like a mud wrestling brawl. It doesn't seem to be a whole lot of fun at first, but once you get into it, you don't really want the action to end. Something I find really fun is when my team works with brands and we find more and more people to add to the "nope!" list. This happened with a particular vacation rental industry client during 2011. Over a three-month period, the client used the "nopes" to more clearly refine who the product was meant to serve and were able to put forth a concise message at launch that:

- Clearly demonstrated an understanding of the audience the company sought to serve.
- Showed the company was doing something in the industry that had never before been done.
- Made the right people sit up and take notice.

When you can see and describe in writing the people who aren't going to be fans of what you're building, it's pretty cool how much clearer your vision of those who will love you becomes.

> *"We like to think of the Us versus Them in terms of a big letter T—the big box competition is the horizontal and we're the vertical. The horizontals of the world, like your Walmarts and Home Depots are interested in selling as many things to as many people for as little as possible and operate on volume. In the vertical, we're offering a specific value-priced set of products—a brand, a lifestyle—to a certain demographic and as deep into that niche as we possibly can."*
> *Source:* Glenda Erwin, Vice President of Marketing, Lehman's

The reality is—and everyone who's built a business that's stood the test of time has had this epiphany—the audience you *think* you serve and the audience who *actually* wants what you have can be very different creatures. By identifying up front the audiences who will be your tough sell, you free yourself up to spend time researching and talking to the audiences who remain after you've crossed these unlikelies off the list.

WHAT GOOD ARE THE TOUGH SELLS?

In throwing out the bathwater, you may be able to save the baby. Some of these "tough sells" may eventually become fans. Others will become your biggest critics. And there are some who'll do what you figured all along might happen: they'll ignore you completely. But the tough sell isn't a primary focus for people looking to build unpopular brands, because they take a lot of energy to keep them in the mix. Spend your energy on the people who will love you, and down the line, the tough sell audience just might find that you really do have something they want.

Understanding who doesn't need you opens up a world of possibilities for you to consider, and chances are pretty good that you'll be left with a bloated list of people who might actually like and use what you want to build. Now, it's time to take that list and narrow it down, so let's talk about some tools that help you hone your audience.

REFINING YOUR AUDIENCE

It may be that the product you want to build fills an absolute void in the market. Or your business expects to be able to offer a savvier set of services or products for an existing audience. Either way, there are some proven strategies for identifying who needs you, determining the value they'll assign to your proposed solution, and learning in greater depth what they consider important. We'll break this down into three areas: competitive analysis, market research, and building avatars.

Competitive Analysis

The top resources for competitive analysis are web searches, press reviews of your competitors' products and services, peer review websites, and industry analysts.

I refer to these sources as snooping. If there are businesses out there that already operate in the space you want to dominate, people are talking about them. *Your* job is to find those conversations. The best tool you have at your disposal is the Internet—just grab your search engine of choice and start keying in search terms that will give you feedback on the brands you want to improve upon:

Love Company X
Hate Company Y
Reviews Company Z

The polarized opinions you'll find in this way are priceless fodder for deciding which audience you ultimately want to serve.

Peer review and rating sites such as Citysearch, OpenTable, Zagat, Yelp, and CNET offer you a powerful cache of information right from the audiences you want to serve. It pays to do a little snooping, especially if you're a brick-and-mortar location, so that you can see what's really resonating with your locale as well as what's consistently mentioned as grounds for improvement. For those developing technology, you can use that sector's reviews to let you know what people are finding buggy or challenging about a competitor's product before you spend the development dollars. Be sure to check out the reviews for particular applications in places like the Android Market or Apple's App Store and do some old-fashioned snooping for "software reviews X" on your competitors' products. Searches like this will also likely lead you to new industry and niche review sites, where you'll have even more consumer feedback information at your fingertips.

You'll also want to search for press coverage and product/service reviews that mention your competition. Start with your competitors' websites and see if they have a Press page. These will generally have links to much of the (positive) press they've received. Then head back to the search engines and see who else has covered them to ensure that you're getting the balanced picture. Noting who has covered your competition can also give you a start on a list of potential publications or news outlets you'd like to see write about your brand someday.

Analysts

Since I'm by no means an expert in working with analysts yet understand how important they've been to multiple clients over the years, I worked with Merredith Branscombe, owner of LEAP! Public Relations (www.leappr.com), to flesh this section out so that you can understand:

- What analysts are.
- Why they're useful.
- Whether or not you need one.
- How to find one.

A huge thanks to Merredith for her insights as a multidecade veteran in the public relations sector.

What Are Analysts, and Why Are They Useful?

What if there were people you could talk to whose only job was to learn about companies just like yours and share that information with people who need it most, such as bigger companies looking to make acquisitions, the media, and other companies looking for sector-specific information)?

Well, you can. Those people are called analysts.

Every product or service sector, from organic packaged goods to Android apps to American plumbing accessories, has its own analysts. Their job is to stay abreast of their particular industry's latest information so that they can share it and on occasion, sell it, to people who would find that information useful. Companies frequently use analysts when looking to acquire new divisions, capabilities, or technologies. These companies contact the leading analysts in the sectors of interest and find out what's hot and what should be on their radar. The media also uses analysts for industry-specific data for everything from newspaper articles to broadcast news.

Given that it's the job of analysts to have a heap of information about a particular sector, they can be especially useful for new businesses and brands for a variety of reasons. Here are just a few insights you can gain from conversations with them about who you are, what you do, and how you do it:

- Other companies you might not know about that are doing something similar.
- Challenges other companies have found in the marketplace with similar technologies.
- How different the analysts perceive your solution from those that already exist.
- Whether what you're doing is exciting given the analyst's knowledge of your industry, which is especially helpful if you're building something with an eye toward being acquired someday.

In many sectors, it's great to be on analysts' radar because it means you can invite them to new product trials and keep them up to date on new developments. There's nothing terrible about getting an insider's thoughts on what you're doing so that you can use that information to better focus your efforts.

But Do I Really Need to Talk to an Analyst?

Maybe, maybe not. If you're an entrepreneur looking to launch a dry cleaning shop or other hyperlocal/local/regional business, the answer is likely no. We've found analysts to be of the most use when our clients are entering very crowded sandboxes like technology. Those developing web/mobile technologies or software will find analysts to be virtually imperative to their business goals. The best way to answer this question, however, is to have a short conversation with a few public relations professionals who specialize in your business's sector and get their feedback. Although you'll get varying answers, you can use the information you gather to determine how important an analyst is to your audience research and then decide on the steps to take to build relationships with him or her.

If I Need an Analyst, How Do I Find One?

Many public relations professionals specializing in sectors where analysts are a key factor—such as the ones mentioned in the technology space—will have built relationships with these experts. That means you should probably reach out to a public relations specialist or firm to assist you in accessing these influencers. And if you think that's too expensive a venture, see the sidebar.

In any case, the simplest way to find an analyst is to go to Google or Bing and type in "analyst" and one of your major (large) competitors. Then look under News section on the search page. Analysts get business from being covered, so look for coverage in the kinds of media *you'd* like to be covered in and see which influencers they're quoting.

If you want to take a direct approach, you can go to one or all of the three leading analyst firm websites: Gartner (www.gartner.com), Forrester Research (www.forrester.com), and Altimeter Group (www.altimetergroup.com). All of these firms have Contact pages that will guide you through the process of connecting with the proper analyst at that firm to meet your needs, as well as the steps you need to take for an introduction. It bears noting that some analyst firms do charge to meet with companies. Although the decision is ultimately yours, there are many options for speaking with qualified professionals if you have a compelling product. Pay-to-play should be on the back burner.

Unpopular brands aren't built by taking shots in the dark. They're built by assembling a powerful team of people who can help you outshine the competition by offering something irresistible to just the right audience. All start-ups, no matter your industry or target demographic, need to allocate resources for public relations and marketing. If you think those are expenses and efforts that can go in the "later" column, I beg to differ.

Why? Many beginning brands powered by incredibly talented and creative people think that having a great product is enough. A great product is nothing without users, though. Marketing efforts—no matter what shape or form they take—have one goal: to acquire users. If you're looking for funding, potential investors want to know you have traction—and traction comes from understanding your niche and learning how to talk to them and entice them to try what you have to offer. And if you're not looking for investors, users have no downside. They're your revenue stream, no matter how you slice it. If you don't spend some effort figuring out how to get their attention, you'll wish you had later on down the road when things aren't moving along as you'd hoped.

MARKET RESEARCH

Market research is commonly associated with big brands and concepts like focus groups, but most brands just getting going don't have the $400 to $700 per head that traditional focus groups cost. So how do you have a conversation with people who fit the demographic you expect to serve and use their input to help shape your brand goals? A great move is to put your boots to the ground and have actual people weigh in on what they think of what you want to build.

For Online Product Concepts

Get your minimally viable product (MVP)—something that ain't necessarily pretty, but works—up and running and invite your friends, colleagues, and coworkers in to poke around. Making a mobile phone app? Developing the next web application to dominate the social media world? Get some people in there using it. Ask them to keep the product under wraps and welcome their feedback with open arms and ears. In the tech start-up community, these early adopters generally turn out to be a valuable resource of any new brand, as they're invested in their own role in shaping something they'll find useful.

For Brick-and-Mortar Concepts

You can't ask your network of friends and coworkers to log in to a test site and hack around, but you still have to find out what it is people love (and don't) about the ideas you have for your business. Tap both people who know you and those who don't; ask your friends and colleagues to recommend anyone they think would be interested in your concept.

- Take a small group on a tour of a few of the places that draw the types of crowd you want to attract. Spend some time in each of these businesses and then meet up at a neutral location afterward. Let them freely share what they did and didn't love about each destination. If you lived in my hometown of Denver and wanted to launch a new brewpub, you might take a tour of the city (by cab!) and check out the Rackhouse Pub, Falling Rock Tap House, Vine Street Pub, and Breckenridge Brewery.
- Do product testing. Host a get-together at your house with the people whose opinions you want and do product testing—whether it's for a new bread recipe or silverware designs being considered for a new restaurant. Product testing is most successful when you let people approach the product on *their* terms and

gauge their reactions. It will also tell you in short order whether people find the things you love to be too complicated or if they aren't using them in the way you thought they might.

Both of these ideas have an infinite number of potential iterations. The point is that you have to get people involved with your product so that they can help you shape its evolution.

And what about online tools? Consider SurveyMonkey, Survey-Gizmo, and GutCheck—three online companies dedicated to helping you understand your audience better than ever.

- **SurveyMonkey (www.surveymonkey.com) and Survey-Gizmo (www.surveygizmo.com):** If you just want to ask a few questions from an existing audience, these two sites offer you the chance to build simple online surveys. What better opportunity for you to leverage an existing e-mail list of loyal customers and clients and up your business's or brand's game? For prices ranging from free to roughly $150 per month, businesses of any size and scale can, in moments, build surveys to get to the heart of whatever it is they want to know from their target demographic. Ask and ye shall receive. *Hint: For social, web-savvy businesses, both of these companies offer their services through Facebook apps. If you have an existing Fan Page, you can activate the app when you're logged into Facebook and get answers from your Facebook community.*

- **GutCheck (www.gutcheckit.com):** Have you ever wanted to have a real-time chat with a 35-year-old male in Illinois who works in the business-to-consumer (B2C) software industry, sports a mullet, and is married with children? Well, GutCheck can find him for you. They're an online qualitative analysis tool that allows brands and companies of any size to interact in real time with people who meet very specific criteria. You can test out brand concepts, logo designs, or packaging concepts or build chats that drill down into why consumers and customers make certain buying decisions. Chats can be anything you want them to be and dig into any part of your business concept you wish; they can also change on the fly. The best part? You're looking at roughly $40 per 30-minute chat to ask some down and dirty questions. If you're building a brand designed to be unpopular, this is your chance to ask questions of the people you figure will never like you. Awesome. *Hint: Use GutCheck to build chats targeting audiences you doubt you'll ever gain business from. They're terrific proving ground for A/B testing. Then take the same concepts and test them with members of your target demographic.*

The information you begin to collect in this stage is a powerful and never-ending resource you'll have at your disposal throughout your brand's development and life span. It will help you shift, refine, distill, and create a brand that your target demographic will embrace and appreciate. And now you know enough about who won't like you, who loves you, and what they find valuable about your solution to paint a picture of who they are.

LET'S MAKE SOME AVATARS

No, it's not a behind-the-scenes look at a James Cameron movie. Jonathan Fields (www.jonathanfields.com), author of *Career Renegade* and *Uncertainty*, says it so well there's no reason for me to rephrase:

> The best way to [envision your ideal customer] is to create an avatar, a detailed persona of the person whose problem you can solve.

We've just figured out what our ideal audience looks like and why they find our solution important, so let's bring them to life—and the process is the same for both real-world, brick-and-mortar businesses and virtual companies. Who would they want to talk to or have dinner with? What kind of chairs (if any at all) would be in the room where you meet? Would these people swear or tell dirty jokes? Do they bring their kids along, or do they leave them with the nanny or, god forbid, in the car? What are their biggest challenges, and what do they value above anything else?

You may find yourself developing multiple avatars that represent the people who need and will love what you're building. It's important, however, to make them human. Like that list you previously developed of all the people who won't like what you're building and why, when you transition from seeing your audience on paper to seeing them as human, you've embraced the first step of building something unpopular—knowing (truly) who you serve.

Consider the modern coffee shop culture. No matter what metropolitan area you live in or visit, you can ask three different people to name the best coffee shop in town and you'll probably get three different answers! Some aspire to be the "coffices" of the world, places where those who traditionally work from home can choose as an alternative to seclusion. Their special sauce might be comfy chairs, breakfast and lunch menus, complimentary WiFi, and electrical outlets galore. They make themselves gathering places. The longer people stay, the more they spend. And then there's the opposite: the coffee shop that doesn't want the all-day campers. Maybe they're catering to the local business scene, and their special sauce consists of a rack of daily papers, a kick-ass chai latte made at warp speed, a few stylish but uncomfortable stools, and a lightning fast cashier—all of which contribute to customers getting their drinks and getting the hell out.

This is the reason we took an entire chapter to identify your audience—because they'll tell you the particular ingredients to use in your brand of secret sauce to keep them around. Creating avatars helps you visualize and better understand the people who will love how it tastes.

Head Exploding . . . Send Help

In roughly 5,000 words, we've gone covered the four steps to figuring out your brand's niche: clarifying, understanding, finding, and building. When you take the time to work through these four steps, you're already miles ahead of everyone out there who is planning on launching some "me too" concept or who thinks they already know exactly what their audience wants. If anything bears repeating at this point, I suppose it would be a quick reminder on the importance of humility.

It's tough to hear people say that they think what you're doing or what you make sucks. But would you rather they *not* tell you and let you hang yourself out to dry before you can even get off the ground? When you take the time to identify the audience you want to serve, the feedback you'll inevitably receive as your brand grows and matures becomes even more valuable. It's straight from the horse's mouth and gives your brand the chance to survive. Being humble keeps us receptive to this kind of feedback. Although it can be hard to take in some instances, it's essential to earning and keeping an audience.

Let's meet a company that learned the hard way about audience identification. Although it's one thing to have an ideal demographic, it's another thing entirely when your ideal demographic doesn't want anything to do with you—at first.

CASE IN POINT: BETTERRIDE

WHEN YOUR AUDIENCE ISN'T YOUR AUDIENCE

This is the story of how a mountain biking instruction company took a digger on its audience concept . . . and kept right on riding.

Colorado is essentially one giant outdoor playground and home to some of the world's most talented athletes in skiing, snowboarding, and multiple cycling disciplines. Gene Hamilton swims in that talent pool.

He discovered snowboarding while in his 20s and continued to compete all the way through college. He ultimately turned professional and took a position as the director of snowboarding at Wisp Resort in Maryland and soon found himself coaching the race team alongside maintaining his own professional snowboarding career. He eventually relocated to Colorado, opting for Breckenridge in order to train with Team Breckenridge and, the following year, Team Tiehack in Aspen. Having never been coached before, Gene noticed that his outlook on the impact of coaching and what it could do for people shifted significantly. It wasn't just about skills; there was a significant mental component to helping people gain confidence and keeping them motivated.

Somewhere around 1993, Gene picked up his first downhill mountain bike. Hooked from the get-go, this already accomplished athlete raced downhill for the next two years as an amateur and turned pro in 1995. Well, in 1996, Gene got his dream job at Steamboat Springs Ski Resort and was named the head snowboard coach. For the next three years, Gene lived his dream as an accomplished athlete in multiple sports, but having spent the past 10 years living in ski towns, he needed a change. He moved to Boulder, Colorado, and decided to combine his love and talent for downhill mountain biking with his love for coaching. He opened BetterRide, Inc., in 1999, a company he envisioned that would work with professional downhill mountain bike racers to help them improve their skills.

But How Big Is Your Audience?

Gene, who has a degree in marketing, did all the right things. He printed hand-to-hand promotional cards that he could distribute at mountain biking events, built a website, and headed out to drum up business. But for all his efforts, the first year of his business netted only two clients. He knew that something wasn't right with his assumptions about his business and that he had to figure out what wasn't working. In the meantime, a handful of people started to find him through various referrals. To keep things going he started teaching anyone who just wanted to learn to ride better. And that's what got him thinking that maybe he'd had his ideal audience wrong from the start. In Gene's words:

> If you look at the numbers in the mountain biking community, [you find that] maybe two percent of mountain bikers actually compete. And of that two percent, maybe twenty percent compete in downhill events. So when I sat down and actually figured out the numbers, I realized my target audience was twenty percent of two percent! On top of that, the average downhill racer is between 12 and
>
> (*continued*)

(continued)

25-years-old and the clients I had coming through the door randomly were averaging 32-years-old or older. When I put all of that together, I thought that maybe I should consider expanding my horizons if I wanted to build a business doing what I loved and a brand that could offer an incredible value for anyone who simply wanted to ride *better*.

Humble Pie—The Perfect Meal for Making the Shift

Gene began teaching the audience he never intended to target, but it was one that was ready, waiting, and asking for what he had to offer. "The biggest enemy in life for anyone is their own ego," says Gene. "Once I got over mine and realized that the audience that wanted what I had to offer was different from the audience I originally *thought* would want it, business started to pick up significantly."

BetterRide went from offering private lessons to multiperson clinics and then expanding into multiday clinics for riders who wanted to develop a deeper skill set. "We were cramming so much information into their heads in a three-hour session that it probably wasn't doing a lot of good. By expanding those clinics to three days from just three hours, we actually gave them time to get comfortable with learning and remember more things they could take back to the trails with them." They were, it seems, developing a way to allow BetterRide to give its newfound audience an even better riding experience— and all it took was a little humility to get there.

Exit Ego, Enter Ideal Audience

Gene knew that his years of experience coaching multiple sports and competing at the professional level gave him a superior product to offer his clientele. The only problem was that he was operating in an ego-driven community. "Mountain biking is a do-it-yourself culture," he explains. "What I realized is if I spent all of my time focusing on converting the egos and making them understand that I could help them get better, I wasn't going to get anywhere."

By taking ego out of the equation, Gene and BetterRide found its ideal audience in the 32-year-old and older demographic. Why? As Gene explains it, "That's when people seem to reach the level of being accepting of assistance. They've been riding or doing whatever it is they've been doing for five, ten years and realize they're not getting any better. That's when people walk through our door. And on top of it, we don't have to sell them anything. They've been looking for us and are ready with eyes and ears wide open to hear and see how we can help them get from where they are to where they want to be."

And the funniest thing happened: Gene is now coaching more and more professional downhill racers. They come to him from various sources, but they all want exactly what Gene has to give: a better ride. When you've reached a certain level in any sport, your body is as fit as it's going to get. That means the only things left to improve upon are skills. By shifting his target audience and building a reputation with every other level of downhill mountain biker, his original audience found their way to his door—and he didn't have to spend all of that time selling to the egos.

Today, BetterRide has 3 full-time staff members and more than 15 contract instructors all across the nation. Gene shares his lesson—one he feels every business owner can benefit from:

> Sometimes business models are too rigid. Sure, sometimes you have to fit into a niche, but if you find something's not working, you might want to consider if you're being too niche with your audience. Stay nimble and shed the ego so you can make a move if your business tells you that you need to make one. You're the only one holding your brand back—and maybe, kinda like I did, you're holding it back from the people who want it most. But don't
>
> *(continued)*

(continued)

confuse the possibility of expanding your reach with taking a shotgun approach. Sometimes it just helps to let your hands off the brakes a little bit. You can keep your focus without losing control.

Better Ride, Inc.
Morrison, Colorado
Website: www.betterride.net
Facebook: www.facebook.com/BetterRide
Twitter: @BetterRide

CHAPTER 3

PERSONALITY

PICK ONE

You're at a dinner party or business mixer—chatting and grabbing a libation or two from the guy who keeps walking by with a tray full of liquid courage. Conversations invariably begin and you share collective miseries about the things we all do in the name of business. You share personal stories. You laugh; you bond. And then a guy walks up to your jovial circle and just stands there, smiling.

You all greet him. "Hello." "What's your name?" "How's it going?" And he launches into asking everyone what he or she does for a living. After he's taken appropriate career inventory, the *spiel* begins. What he does, how it can help everyone, and before long, your jovial group comes up with lame excuses one by one and everyone scatters, desperate to get away from That Guy.

DON'T BE THAT GUY

People do business with people. If you don't believe me, think about the last five business transactions you made and how you feel about the people who were your main point of contact. Dollars to donuts, you liked the people (at least on some level) who were involved with the transaction. We're part of a business culture that makes decisions based on relationships, and it's damn near impossible to establish a relationship with That Guy.

That Guy is interested in one thing: himself. He could not care less about what's important to you, either as a person or a consumer. He's looking to make a sale, not build a relationship. That Guy is the epitome of the brand and company you never want to become, because he's missing a personality.

WHAT MAKES UP A BRAND'S PERSONALITY?

Think about your closest friend in the world—values, nuances, favorite phrases, what he's great at (and sucks at), the sound of his voice and inflection, what riles him up and how he relaxes, and things that make him laugh and how he makes you laugh.

Brands aren't one-dimensional logos built from vector graphic images and Pantone colors. They aren't products. The wildly unpopular ones—those who find traction, success, and longevity—are the ones that act like people. They're living, breathing beings made up of four distinct parts, and the sooner you accept that, the sooner you can leave all of Those Guys behind in the dust.

Let's look at the four parts of building a brand's personality:

- **The Who:** People do business with people, so how can you make your brand human?
- **Growing a Pair:** Brands, like people, have opinions and you shouldn't be afraid to let those be known. We'll also discuss road kill and how to avoid becoming it.
- **Emotional Aspects of Brand Personality:** How to acknowledge what's important to your audience and build a persona they'll love.
- **Practical Aspects of Brand Personality:** This is the visual representation of your brand. When you know who you are, it's a lot easier to communicate that without words. And if you've hired a graphic designer before going through the three previous steps, I'll kick your ass.

Before we get going on the four steps, I think we have a lesson or two we could learn from a giant robot dinosaur on personality.

In late September 2011, I stumbled across a post on Fred Wilson's blog (www.avc.com). Fred's an influential member in the venture capitalist community, and I'm a frequent reader of his blog due to my work in the technology start-up sector. Tuning in for what I thought was going to be my daily dose of start-up sensibility, I instead found the best explanation of the importance of brand personality conveyed in a most creative way: a blog and a cartoon drawn by a giant robot dinosaur named FAKEGRIMLOCK. (Who knew that imaginary giant robot dinosaurs wrote blogs?)

The first iterations of products are commonly referred to as MVPs, or minimum viable products. Grimmy took another twist on this common term in the tech sector and wrote a post about minimum viable personality, something brands in every sector can get a grip on.

Minimum Viable Personality

MOST IMPORTANT STEP FOR BUILD PRODUCT IS BUILD PRODUCT.

SECOND MOST IMPORTANT IS BUILD PERSONALITY FOR PRODUCT.

NO HAVE PERSONALITY? PRODUCT BORING, NO ONE WANT.

PERSONALITY BETTER THAN MARKETING

WHEN CHOOSE PRODUCT, HUMANS ONLY CARE ABOUT DOES WORK, AND IS INTERESTING.

WORLD ALREADY FULL OF THINGS DO WORK. MOST BORING.

PERSONALITY = INTERESTING. INTERESTING = CARE. CARE = TALK.

EVERYONE CARE AND TALK ABOUT PRODUCT? YOU WIN.

(continued)

(continued)

SELL TO FRIENDS, NOT STRANGERS

PERSONALITY MAKE PRODUCT FRIEND. YOU HELP FRIEND. YOU FORGIVE WHEN FRIEND NOT PERFECT. YOU WANT FRIEND WIN.

BORING STRANGER? . . . YOU NOT.

PERSONALITY IS API FOR LOYALTY. NO ONE CARE WHICH BORING STRANGER IS NEXT. BUT ALWAYS WANT FRIEND NEXT.

NO FORGET LOYALTY PORT

PERSONALITY MAKE MEANING

CAN PET ROCK. PET DOG BETTER. PET DOG HAVE MEANING.

BORING PRODUCT IS ROCK. NO HAVE MEANING. INTERACT WITH PERSONALITY DIFFERENT. HAVE MEANING.

INTERESTING PRODUCT THAT GIVE FRIENDS MEANING = MOST WIN OF ALL.

THIS IS NOT A ROCK

HOW NOT BE BORING

HAVE PERSONALITY EASY. ANSWER THREE QUESTIONS:

1. HOW YOU CHANGE CUSTOMER'S LIFE?

2. WHAT YOU STAND FOR?

3. WHO OR WHAT YOU HATE?

NOW HAVE MISSION, VALUES, ENEMY. THAT ENOUGH FOR MINIMUM VIABLE PERSONALITY.

KEEP IN BRAIN WHEN WRITE, TALK, BLOG, TWEET. ITERATE. IMPROVE WHAT WORK. DELETE WHAT NOT. PERSONALITY GROW.

NO BE CHICKEN

CHICKEN LIVE IN CAGE. NO CAN HAVE PERSONALITY INSIDE CAGE.

LAST STEP IS SMASH CAGE, LIGHT BARN ON FIRE.

DO THAT, YOU WIN.

NO ONE GOING TO EAT THIS CHICKEN

(continued)

Neither you nor I is an imaginary giant robot dinosaur who writes in all caps and broken English. But we should all offer FAKEGRIMLOCK a collective high five for giving us a humorous, personality-laden, and incredibly accurate introduction as to why personality is your brand's first responsibility behind your product.

YOUR BRAND IS A WHO

When my online presence began emerged back in 2006, it was simply Redheaded Fury—a site for all of my early-30s angst to come out. When I started blogging for business not long after, I kept those thoughts on a separate site, Redhead Writing. I was fairly sure that my friends weren't interested in my online business tips and the people in my professional world probably didn't want to hear my thoughts on demons, swings, and sunflowers. It was okay for *me* to have an opinion, but I didn't think it was appropriate to let my business audience see it.

I kept this separation of church and state going until one day a colleague asked me, "Why isn't your name anywhere on your websites?" I just said that it wasn't really important who I was—what was important was what I *did*. She promptly called bullshit on that, saying that she felt that I, Erika, was my brand, and that should be placed front and center, as my audience needed to see that there was a person fueling them.

But I'm a jumper; in other words, if it's new and there could be value in it for my business, I'm game to try it. In early 2010, I relaunched a new website design (Erika Napoletano is Redhead Writing) and also combined both sites (Redheaded Fury and Redhead Writing) into one. My audience loved it (I ate some crow), and I found my business readers quickly jumping over and commenting on my more personal blogs and vice versa. When I became a unified front—a single human being who produces all of these ideas—*that's* when my brand really started to grow. My audience attached my thoughts—business and personal—to an actual human being, not just words on the page.

My audience continues to tell me that the reason they keep coming back to read my blogs and share their thoughts is because I'm an f-bomb-loving, mince-no-words broad who has a knack for poking fun at herself. I've put out a welcome mat that allows them to become a part of my stories, see themselves in my own foibles, and not be afraid to disagree with me on occasion.

I'm human.

I've built relationships with my readers using the same tools we use to build friendships with people. There's a learning curve when we meet someone new; you have to see how you fit into that person's story and how he or she fits into yours. If you weren't a fan of unpopular thoughts and blunt advice, you probably weren't going to be around my neck of the woods for long. My audience initially stopped by for the what, found that they liked the who delivering the message, and over time, and the who—not the what—was the glue that kept them coming back.

Your brand is a who. It's *never* a what. I don't care if you're a blogger slinging words on a computer keyboard or manufacturer of microchips. It doesn't matter if you consider yourself a personal or corporate brand. People do business with people, and brands that help their audience understand that there's a person behind the pitch have the opportunity to soar far above the rest.

If you're not a fan of what I say and how I say it, chances are you're not going to be a fan of how I do business, communicate, or shop for produce, for that matter. It's the question I answer most often in interviews: "Do you ever lose business on account of your outspoken voice?" The answer is yes—every single day! At first, it made me whine, *Why can't people accept my brand for what it can deliver and how it can help them?* Now, I operate with the knowledge that the people who accept it, appreciate it, and are inspired by my brand are the ones I want to do business with. You need to accept that and stop being afraid to leave money on the table because someone or some company doesn't like or agree with something you said.

LEAVING MONEY ON THE TABLE

The most important thing businesses can do is understand and own up to the type of business they don't want to attract. And yes, when you're starting out, it's common to take everything that crosses your threshold because people are willing to write checks. Your brand personality helps you attract the right audience and send the wrong ones packing.

WHICH BRINGS US TO PISSING PEOPLE OFF . . .

Brands should be inherently human. If you remember only one thing from this chapter, let it be this: you and your friends share many things that make your relationships work, but you don't always agree. Sometimes you're flat-out twisted at one another, and it takes communication, understanding, and maybe a drink or two to get over it. Brands are no different. Just as you're not friends with everyone, your brand won't be either. But unpopular brands aren't afraid to pick a side, because they know what's important, what they stand for, and what they're willing to walk away from in pursuit of what's most important to their business goals.

Right now, get over the fear that you're going to offend someone. It's going to happen, even when it's not your intention. Great brands understand that and then put their energy into triaging that feedback, because human beings (well, rational ones) have conversations where people don't always agree and then have to deal with those situations and move on.

Here's what your brand personality will do for your business:

- Define who you are and why you do what you do.
- Consistently reinforce that you're not here to please everyone and keep you on track to make decisions that will honor your audience while nurturing your business goals.
- Remind you to stand by those decisions and take any required heat for them.
- Keep you human, which occasionally involves eating crow or shifting strategy, something every successful brand finds necessary along the way.

Remember the avatars you created for your audience in Chapter 2? You have to create an avatar for your business as well—you have to build its personality. When you can enumerate all of the things that make your brand human, you'll find it a lot easier to have an opinion. And I'm not going to lie—building a brand personality and its avatar includes making some tough decisions about who you'll be and what you'll say and ultimately owning those words and actions. Your brand personality dictates how you'll manage everything from success to conflict, and you're going to need to get some thick skin to deal with those and everything in between.

GROWING A PAIR—THE CORE OF PERSONALITY

Do you think people want to do business with a brand they know they can walk all over? Doubtful. The business world has no dearth of brands that lose focus on their personality and abandon their audience midstream (*cough, cough,* Netflix, anyone?); you're not looking to be one of them. Unpopular brands have grown a pair and aren't afraid of being unapologetically honest about who they are and what they believe. And there are multiple benefits to showing this kind of bravery:

- **Audience Expectations:** People like to know what to expect from brands. Growing a pair means sticking to your principles, especially when it's to the benefit of your audience. Think about things like fair trade manufacturing practices, commitments to sustainability, and your return policy. These are your brand values and things you're passionate about. People have passion, and you can't have passion without a pair to back it up.

- **Rising Above:** There is crap that's pervasive in every industry. Growing a pair allows you to rise above. Again, it doesn't mean being a jerk. It means having the gumption to follow the straight and narrow and respect your audience enough to not engage in the stuff you scoop out of the litter box. Your pair lets you avoid less-than-productive conversations and conduct business on a higher level than brands that think bickering with their audience or competitors is a viable strategy.
- **Integrity:** Growing a pair gives you permission to conduct business with integrity. You don't flip-flop or waver. You set your course and follow it with intent. Maybe you call this determination. But it's still having a pair and letting your audience know what you will and won't tolerate when it comes to how you've met their expectations.

Look back at the last time you shared a meal with more than one person. Did everyone around the table agree on everything in every conversation that arose during the course of that meal? If so, remind me never to come to one of your dinner parties, because they're probably held in Wonderland, and that's not a commute I'm willing to make. People disagree on things every day, and as a brand, you're no different. If you're looking to do business with more than one person, ever, you're going to find someone who begs (or yells) to differ. Playground politics told us that we had to please everyone, bring enough Bubble Yum to share with the rest of the class, and find some mythical level of unanimous acceptance. In business, it's very much a different story.

Running an unpopular brand means you understand that everyone isn't your friend, nor will they be; but your friends and the people with whom you have something in common are your most important assets. Your personality makes you approachable (which we cover in Chapter 4). Approachable people have more friends. Brands need friends and need to be a friend to their audience. And all of my friends have opinions; I'll bet yours do, too.

A BIT ON ROAD KILL

We met Merredith Branscombe back in Chapter 2 when we were talking about analysts. She has a way of explaining the importance of taking a stand to her clients that is entirely applicable to how you approach your brand's personality. I asked her to share the "talk" she gives clients when she's prepping them to speak with the press—it backs up why that pair you're growing is going to come in handy.

We've all been taught to be political and neutral. We're taught to construct sentences so that they cause no tremors of disagreement, no discord, no hurt feelings. So when my startups hear that they are going to be plopped in front of the *Wall Street Journal* or *TechCrunch*, and I ask them a sample question to see how they'll potentially respond, they often choose the most careful answer they can. They don't want to be wrong. They use $10 words and the best marketing-speak a business school education can buy. That's the best way to answer, right?

Wrong.

If you want to be considered an expert, someone who's worthy of an audience's attention, then you must have an opinion. That doesn't mean you disregard the facts. It means you've considered and analyzed them (and you can even reference them) and you have an opinion because you are informed and you follow what's happening in this field.

It's not bad. People need opinions, even when they don't agree with them, because other people's opinions are what help you crystallize your own. When you are quoted in the media, you are held out implicitly as an expert in your industry or field, and most of your peers will respect that (or envy it), even if they disagree.

And here's a bit of a secret: if you want to be quoted for your expertise, few media types want to hear—or have time or space to print—someone's carefully worded, neutral answer. If you want to be quoted, pick a side of the road, commit to it, then get out of the way.

The middle of the road—that's where you get run over. So if you want to be road kill, stick to the middle. Otherwise, figure out a great way to express your opinion, make sure you can back it up—maybe practice it a couple of times if you get nervous—and get out there.

And are there situations where you need to not have an opinion as a brand? Most definitely. Merredith weighs in on those as well:

There are a couple of exceptions where you *don't* want to offer an opinion.

- **If you're an executive at a publicly traded company:** Imagine someone says, "How are things looking this quarter?" Guess what? People have gone to jail for expressing opinions like these. The correct answer is, "Oh, you'll have to tune in to our quarterly earnings call to find out." And then you change the subject.
- **If your company is in crisis:** This is when it's time to sublimate your own personal opinions ("That customer was an idiot") and, more than likely, work with an attorney and a PR professional you trust to see what, if anything, you need to say, how to say it, and when. There aren't that many times when it's appropriate to write by committee, but this is one of them. "The company issued a statement . . . " is perfectly appropriate here.
- **If you're in a public forum and making an accusation against a specific individual in a fixed medium:** Have an opinion? You'd better be able to back it up; otherwise laws regarding defamation may come into play, and that's a very expensive opinion.

So we know that brands are human and that humans have opinions—albeit the few cases where they're not meant to be expressed. Not everyone's going to like them; only the right people should be picking up what you're putting down. So how do you use the information you gathered about your ideal audience and niche in Chapter 2 and apply it to building a personality they'll love?

MOVE ME (PLEASE)—THE EMOTIONAL ASPECTS OF PERSONALITY DEVELOPMENT

Remember the jovial circle of people chatting earlier before That Guy came along? They were talking about business, life, and the nuances of what makes life worth living. That's how people build relationships; they find things in common. We laugh, commiserate, cry, and debate, and through those experiences, we find people who make our lives more fulfilling. Just as one person can't force his or her way into being our be-all, end-all, a company can't shoehorn its way into an audience. You have to build relationships with your target audience, which you do by letting the human side bubble to the surface. It's the "loyalty port" that FAKEGRIMLOCK spoke of. Relationships give you access to your audience's loyalty port, and we build them by paying enough attention to our audience to understand what frustrates them—and then we actively take steps to avoid being a part of their frustrations!

WHAT DO YOU WANT TO MAKE YOUR CUSTOMERS FEEL?

There's no brand out there that wants their target audience to feel like crap. You also don't want to make your audience feel "good," because good isn't a word that you can work with. It's not even really a feeling. You have to dig a bit deeper into your brand's personality—so far we've covered being human and having opinions—so that you can develop the avatar for your brand.

Our friends run the entire spectrum of personality traits. Some are quick-witted and always ready with a joke; others are dry and occasionally morose. We have friends who swear a blue streak and others who think whispering *mother of pearl* is edgy. The one thing they all have in common (hopefully) is that when you're around them, *you don't feel crappy*. So what do these people do that make you feel *not crappy?*

- **Listen:** Some friends are better listeners than others, but a successful brand has to be an extremely talented listener.

Think about the friend who has this talent and how that person lets you know that he or she is plugged into you. That's the friend you call when things are down, and this friend is ready and waiting to lend you an ear. We feel less burdened by what bothers us when people listen. When people give us their attention, we feel validated, worthy, that our ideas and thoughts have merit.

- **Offer help:** Certain friends are our go-tos for various things—home repairs, the perfect black top to borrow for a night out, tools you don't have in your garage. They are willing to help us out with what we need, and some even offer their help before we know we need it. It's a great relief—knowing that someone with expertise can help us get something done. It gives us a much-needed sense of security—being able to tap into someone we know and trust for assistance.

- **Make us laugh:** Our crack-up friends are so incredibly valuable. They say everything we wish we could (but can't) and help us take a break from our daily routines. They're ready with a joke, funny picture, or funny video, and they remind us to not take ourselves too seriously. Laughter is a proven psychological and physiological release.

- **Nurture:** Ah, and then there are the friends who are the caretakers, planners, and boosters. They can show us the way from point A to B and have all the details worked out in between. They offer a familiar port or even a hug when needed (yes, even the dudes). They host Sunday football with a fridge full of beer and point out to you everything you're doing right. These friends are our destressors, and all entrepreneurs need them in their lives. They help us hold it together and keep it fun.

Besides its own particular quality, each of these personality traits evokes a shared emotion—a feeling of *relief*. That's what we get from our friends, and when you're deciding what type of personality you want your brand to have, think about how you'll be the harbor in the storm—welcome relief—for that ideal audience.

Your personality—it's the human fuel behind your brand and what will allow you to greet your audience (approachability), make your audience want to introduce you to new people (sharability), bring all of those new people to your door so that you can grow and find the team you need to accommodate this awesome growth (scalability), and then make sure that you're not working for too little or free (profitability). There's a reason personality was the first thing we covered—it's the first thing people will meet aside from your product and what makes them feel comfortable once they've met you at the marketing cocktail party.

Unpopular brands make their audience feel. And it's not until you begin to understand the way you want your brand's personality to make your audience feel that should you start thinking about the practical presentation of your brand.

You have permission to call your graphic designer now.

PUTTING IT ON PAPER: THE PRACTICAL ASPECTS OF BRAND PERSONALITY

There's more to a great brand than a logo and a website. All too often, business owners get so gung ho about having a physical destination and representation of their brand that they pull the trigger too early. Here are just a few reasons why I was going to kick your ass if you hired a graphic designer before you got to this step:

- **Wasted Money:** Coming up with brand concepts, designing logos, trademarking, and website development aren't cheap processes. I work with way too many start-ups and young businesses that have built physical representations of their brands that don't reflect anything about the audience they seek to serve. And the reason is because they haven't done their homework. Save your money and spend it right the first time. It doesn't mean your brand can't evolve; it just means you have a better chance of getting the visual aspects right the first time.
- **Audience Confusion:** Ever showed up at the website for a brand you know and trust and suddenly everything looks different? Many companies go through rebranding processes over time, but the last thing you want to do is confuse your audience right out of the gate by showing them too many looks in too

short a period. Get to know yourself before you jump in and tell everyone who you are.

- **Misdirected Focus:** When you're testing a new business concept or product, you need to spend time on the business itself or else you won't need a flashy logo. Worry about getting an MVP and something that people can sink their teeth into. The same people will be ready to give you feedback on logo variations and website designs once they understand what you have to offer and how it applies to them. How will they know if a website concept or logo fits your company if they don't know how—or whether—what you have to offer fits their lives?

By taking the steps to understand who your brand is from intellectual (values, ethics, mission) and emotional (how you want your audience to feel around this brand) standpoints, you'll have better information with which to shape the physical manifestations of your brand. And you'll avoid wasting time and money on things that you'll have to do over again. When building your brand's physical personality, it's imperative to find the right creative professionals to help you get it done.

- **Do your research:** What do graphic designers cost in your market? What's the differential between freelancers and agency rates? Ask colleagues who have gone through a similar process what they paid and help yourself establish a realistic budget for your visual branding needs.
- **Establish a budget:** You'll find graphic designers who charge anywhere from $35 to more than $100 per hour. Many offer project rates, and others charge by the hour. Know how much you have allocated for your visual branding and share this information with your candidates. If they can't work for that, say thank you and move on.
- **Get referrals:** Look for brands with the same type of personality you're looking to develop and ask who did their work. Most graphic designers have a particular style (kinda like the brand you're building), and there's nothing wrong with that. Look for

one who already creates the type of look you're going for rather than one whose work you think is visually compelling but not your style.

- **Remember that you don't need everything right now:** Business cards? Probably. Letterhead, fancy envelopes, and a metric ton of other printed items with your logo all over it? Probably not. You can avoid printing costs of letterhead by having your graphic designer create a digital letterhead that you can print on the paper of your choice. Envelopes can be plain. With so much business being done electronically these days, avoid printing costs unless it's absolutely necessary. Even investor kits can be electronic, and your prospective investors will probably appreciate digital copies they can flip through on their iPads on a plane. Even trade show collateral can be e-mailed to booth visitors—then they won't lose it or leave it at the hotel!

When you decide on the right designer or agency to help you with your brand's visual personality, do that person a solid and give him or her examples of what you like and why. No, they're not going to rip it off—it helps them get their bearings on your expectations and style preferences.

The same goes for website designers. Make sure you get referrals and establish your budget. WordPress is the most popular platform for building websites these days, and developers are in plentiful supply. When you find sites you like, check the footer (the very bottom of the home page) for design credits and links. That makes it easier to connect and explore potential designers in a timely fashion.

And for anyone you're entrusting to build the visual personality for your brand, have a full discovery meeting and explain who you are and what the visual marks should convey. Forget e-mail—it's time for in-person meetings or Skype video conference. Personality is too precious to trust to e-mail when it's in the developmental stages. Use that pair you grew awhile back to set up some face time with the people who are going to help you become who you need to be to best serve your audience, and let them get to know *your* personality in the process!

ARE WE DONE?

No. You're never done with your brand's personality. In the same way that you're not the same person you were when you were 14 years old, your brand's personality will keep evolving. Our take-aways from this chapter are that your brand is a living being and can make mistakes. We find the humanity in brands that own up to those mistakes and aren't above saying "oops" occasionally. Along the way you'll undoubtedly learn more about what's important to your audience, and you can start (that's right, I said *start*) refining how to present your brand visually.

Since we started this discussion of personality with some compelling ideas from a giant robot dinosaur, we might as well finish with a truck in Seattle that lives every aspect of FAKEGRIMLOCK's blog post. I met the folks featured in the following case study while working on my *Entrepreneur Magazine* column. Although the interview for that article was on a completely different subject, the approach they took to their brand's personality shone through in everything they did. Enjoy meeting Roz, Kamala, and Emily as we take a look at Marination—one truck, one storefront, and enough personality to fill both and beyond.

CASE IN POINT: MARINATION
SERVING UP ALOHA EVERY DAY

How do you cheer up a city that averages only 56 days of sunshine amidst more than 220 days of cloud cover each year? That's what the founders of Marination Mobile asked before they ever launched their Hawaiian fusion food truck business in 2009. They knew one thing was for certain from the get-go: personality would be a key player in the customer-facing curbside cuisine business, so they'd better make theirs one to remember. Sure, people take walks in the rain, but if you're going to venture out of the office and maybe get soaked, your destination better have more than zippy tacos.

Just a few short years later, Marination Mobile's been mentioned in more regional and national magazines than its website's media page can hold and has been invited to the Food Network's Great Food Truck Challenge for both 2010 and 2011. Read on and find out how this hyperlocal brand's sunny disposition keeps their customers coming back for more and created the need for a brick-and-mortar location a mere 12 months after they took the parking brakes off their food truck on opening day. Cofounder Kamala Saxton gives us the scoop on the emotional side of their tasty brand:

> Neither my partner, Roz, nor I came from the restaurant industry, so we [knew that if] were going to move forward with this idea of launching a food truck business, we had to know that there was going to be some sort of financial reward. When we crunched the numbers and saw that it could be profitable, we thought, "What's going to make people keep coming back when there are all these other food trucks to choose from?" For us, the answer was simple: our personality. We knew that we had to bake personality in from the very beginning, so we built our business and marketing strategies with a pretty substantial line item for marketing and branding.
>
> ### We Don't Skimp on Ingredients, So Why Skimp on Marketing Budget?
>
> It's not hard to see that a lot of businesses starting up or floundering around have skimped on their marketing budget. Whether you think that word of mouth alone is going to carry you or think marketing is an unnecessary expense, you're wrong. When you're building a business that needs feet in front of it each and every day, marketing is the one thing you can't afford to skimp on. Marination doesn't skimp on ingredients in their food, so they don't skimp on marketing either. It's an equally

(continued)

(*continued*)

important ingredient, which is where personality comes
into play.

Your Customers Aren't Stupid

When Marination's founders were determining how to best
communicate the brand's personality, they knew one of the
most important things on their plate would be finding the
right employees to express it. If you have employees who deal
with customers, they're going to inevitably be the face of your
brand personality. It doesn't matter if you're witty and charm-
ing when you use social media. If you're as interesting as a box
of rocks when people actually show up to spend money,
the chances that they'll become repeat customers are slim.
Marination knew that people aren't stupid and can tell
what's real and what's not. That's why they built Marination
around not only delicious Hawaiian-Korean cuisine but also
employees who communicate that message while serving the
food each day.

Before they even launched, Kamala and Roz were fortunate
enough to meet Emily Resling, their social marketing chief.
She's helped shape the brand from its beginnings and is the
voice of Marination's online brand today. Some companies
might be hesitant to let their employees have so much control
of their brand's voice, fearing that if the employees leave, they'll
have to try to replicate that personality. There's an easy way to
take care of that, though. In Marination's case, Emily's designed
a style guide for how the brand behaves online. What they
sound like, what they like, things that are important to them—
it's all in there. So if, heaven forbid, Emily moves on, Marination can pass the torch to the next person. "And you know
what's great?" asks Kamala. "If and when that time comes, that
person will bring their personality into the one we've already
built and it can only get better."

Spreading the Message

You must make your brand personality distinct and clear with your own employees before anyone on the outside is ever going to pick up on it and come to love it. "We always make sure that everyone in our company knows what's going on with our marketing efforts. It's part of the way we serve up aloha every day," Kamala explains. A well-informed staff never makes anyone feel silly for not knowing what's going on. Marination's customers are then better served and leave happy, which means they're coming back happy the next time they see their truck roll up.

How "Serving Up Aloha" Shines through the Seattle Crowds

"We're in a market that's got its share of dreary weather, so we developed our brand personality to be a bright spot in each of our customers' days," says Kamala. They hear time and time again from customers about their Order Takers' uncanny ability to remember names and orders day after day. They see messages posted on Facebook and Twitter that one of their customers saw Kamala at the recent U2 concert or saw one of their Order Takers out and about town. One of their Order Takers was recently featured in the local paper, and Marination's customers showed up at the store and the truck with newspaper clippings and congratulations for her. That's not something that happens with a crappy brand personality. These are the people who *are* Marination's brand. "As a business owner," Kamala says, "this is what tells me we've hit it out of the park."

Marination set out to build a brand personality that was alive both online and in person, and here are some of the ways they've communicated that from the very beginning:

- **Prelaunch:** "We thought we were about two months from rolling out the food truck for the first time, and we

(continued)

(*continued*)

didn't really have any news to share," Kamala remembers. "So we built a playlist of songs that our customers would be hearing when they came to visit us when we opened. Our Twitter handle is @curb_cuisine, so Emily took pictures of nice-looking curbs and tweeted them out along with special notes to each one of our followers in the pre-opening days. The funky, kooky, personalized notes from non-restaurant industry 'mystery people' who were launching a food truck were a big hit. Lots of folks wanted to talk to us before we even had anything to say. We had a distinct online personality (and a couple hundred people familiar with it) before we ever served our first taco."

- **Focus:** There's a reason Marination has only one truck; it's a matter of building their brand so that they can best serve their customers. Consistency with a brand personality is huge. Kamala states that they believe that if they had multiple trucks instead of just one truck and their new storefront location, it would be a lot harder to keep their brand image and personality consistent.

- **Communication:** Marination's customers can find them in one of four places: Facebook, Twitter, the storefront location, or the truck. It's pretty simple. If they have a problem, complaint, or praise, Marination's on it with a response, apology, or thanks. One customer recently tweeted that the tortillas were a bit burnt one day, and Marination was right there, out in the open, fessing up and inviting her back with a comp. "She was right!" said Kamala. "The tortillas were a bit burnt that day, and we own that."

When Marination opened its storefront location, they had customers who would tweet or post on Facebook that they couldn't find them. Well, Kamala would walk out of the store and down to the corner, waving her arms around so that they *could* find them. "If they were going to take the time to tell us they were trying to find us, I was going to help them do it!" she shares. "No matter what our customers have to say, we're ready to hear it, and now our customers are even bringing us suggestions. We love that! Our personality is friendly, and customers know our aloha spirit means their ideas and feedback are welcome."

- **Goodwill:** This is a powerful example of brand personality in action. "There are some days where our credit card machine doesn't work," Kamala offers. "While rare, we're not going to penalize our card-carrying customers for it. We can't take the card, they don't have cash, so we give them an IOU (they owe us) with their food. They come back the next time we're on their block, and they hand us the IOU funds *and* their payment for their next order. We were recently waiting in line for the ferry to one of the islands with the truck, on our way to cater an event. Here comes a girl walking up to us, and we could see she had money in her hand and we're thinking, 'Oh man, I hope she doesn't think we're serving food here in the ferry line!' Well, it turns out that she had been at our truck over a year ago and we'd given her an IOU for her order. She handed over $7: 'Five dollars for the IOU and $2 for interest. Thank you!'" Marination lives the aloha spirit every day, and their customers? Seems they live it in return!

- **Brand Growth:** As they start to do more corporate catering, weddings, and other events where people aren't coming directly to either the truck or the store, Marination has to find ways to make their personality shine through in these new business environments. In these cases, it's their employees. Hiring the right people who bring that friendly, helpful, personalized aloha spirit to situations where the biggest pieces of our branding aren't present is crucial. They've employ people who make sure that no matter how far away people are from the truck or store, they know without even tasting the food that Marination is catering that event.

(*continued*)

(*continued*)

- **Brand Philanthropy:** Marination's founders built the brand so that their customers and the community alike know that they're a very giving brand. A portion of the company's revenues go to support the Susan G. Komen Foundation, and they're incredibly active in the community. "For the second year in a row, we were invited to participate in the Food Network's Great Food Truck Challenge, and for the second year, we'll decline," Kamala explains. "It comes down to the fact that we have one truck and one storefront, and those two places are where our customers need us to be. The contest would take us on the road and away from our customers—the people who generate our revenue—for up to five weeks, and that's just not good business. Instead, we're using our brand's marketing power to support three other food trucks from Seattle who are competing for a win online and a spot on the show. You can't be stingy with your brand and make it all about you. We're the brand that wants to help our customers and the Seattle community because that's what good people do. It's also what great brands do."

The Many Layers of Personality

Just like people, brand personalities have a lot of layers. From Marination's snappy, upbeat, and friendly online presence to their Order Takers and involvement in the community, they make sure that it all comes together in one concise message. They hire the right people, respond to their customers, and do everything they can to be that food truck you want to hang out with! And for them, it's easy, because it's who they are and who their employees are, and they attract the customers who like who they are. "We sell $2.25 tacos," Kamala states. "To keep people coming back, we have to offer more than that. Our personality keeps them tuned in for what's next, no matter if they're tuning in online or in person."

Takeaway Tips for Any Business

- **Be genuine.** Your customers aren't stupid and can pick fake out of a lineup.
- **Be consistent.** When people aren't consistent with their behavior, we call them crazy. You don't want to have a crazy brand personality. Make sure you're seen as the same brand—and persona—in every venue where you market.
- **Don't underestimate the power of social media.** If it's the right thing for your industry or niche, you can't pretend it doesn't exist. Your personality can really shine through in those venues, especially if you have the right person behind it. You can reach so many more people and have so many more conversations. It's one of the cornerstones of our brand's success.
- **Choose employees carefully and inform them.** Every person you hire should reflect your brand personality. Keep them informed of your marketing and branding efforts and give them buy-in. When your employees understand that you trust them with your brand, you'll be surprised how much you can learn from them about what you can do to make your business more successful.
- **Allocate resources to build your brand's personality.** Don't skimp on the marketing budget. Yeah, it might hurt to put that money aside and it's not cheap by any means, but it pays you back so many times over. Spend it wisely and hire the right people who live to be your brand. You won't regret it.

Marination
Seattle, Washington
Website: www.marinationmobile.com
Facebook: www.facebook.com/marinationmobile
Twitter: @curb_cuisine

CHAPTER 4

APPROACHABILITY
PUTTING OUT THE WELCOME MAT

Now that you're on the way to creating a brand personality that speaks to your target audience and that you can hone and refine over time, it's time to use it to encourage that audience to communicate with you.

Whatever your brand offers and no matter whom it's built to serve, today's business climate gives your audience unprecedented power. Let's explore some of the changes that have recently taken place in marketing and branding culture and how they affect your brand's ability to create ongoing conversations with your audience.

A SHIFT TO INBOUND MARKETING

Vintage magazine ads and commercials from the 1950s through the 1990s provided for only one-way conversations. Printed media, television, and radio were the primary outlets the public relied on to learn about new products and services. Marketing-speak was broadcast to the public. There weren't 800 numbers. Websites with contact forms and e-mail addresses didn't even exist. Brands spoke and customers listened—whether we wanted to or not—in order to get to the programming on the other side of the advertising.

Flash forward to 1999, when digital video recorders (DVRs) like TiVo and ReplayTV were introduced. It was the beginning of the end for TV commercials. Then in 2001, satellite radio launched, marking the beginning of the end for radio advertising. Today, you can fast-forward through, flip past, or simply ignore any advertising message you don't want to receive.

Brands couldn't sneak into your car or living room anymore. They had to ask permission. That permission was granted only by consumers who wanted to hear your marketing messages and allowed you into their inboxes, on their radios, and on their televisions. Even magazines have gone digital, letting us access articles online and skip the full-page ads. Today's culture sounds a lot like, "If I don't want a brand in my face, they're not going to get any face time!" This permission-based, or inbound, marketing has turned over the communications process to the customer, and it's the brand's responsibility to listen and respond.

Customers now tell brands, "Hey, I'd like to hear more. Come on inside." So how do we get invited inside? Here's where personality comes into play.

PERSONALITY UNLOCKS APPROACHABILITY

Your audience is talking, everywhere, it seems, and nonstop. They're telling you what they want, how much they'll pay for it, and what color they want it to come in. They'll tell you what they need and when they need it, too. You developed a brand personality so that your business comes across as someone that your audience actually wants to talk to. They're talking anyway—making your brand *approachable* allows your audience to feel comfortable sharing those conversations with you, inviting you inside their thoughts and feelings.

FOUR THINGS

Yeah, I make a lot of lists—five components of the unpopular brand, four steps for audience identification. Lists give us something concrete to check our progress against. So let's check and see if the unpopular brand you're building hits all four principles that'll make it approachable and give you access to your audience's prized yearnings and concerns.

- **The Welcome Mat:** It's about letting your audience know you understand them, that you're ready and willing to converse, and that you invite (and are grateful for) their feedback.
- **Your Brand Story:** It's the combination of personality, product offering, and how these intersect with your audience. Your story needs to convey a rationale for you all belonging together and make your audience feel like they're a part of what it is you're doing.
- **Elevation of Your Audience:** There is no other reason in this world to create a brand and its associated product or service offerings than to serve your audience. This is why unpopular brands show an inordinate amount of respect for their

audiences and aren't afraid to indulge in the occasional necessary mea culpa.

- **Protocols for Response:** That sounds fancy, doesn't it? If your audience is talking, you need to have basic practices in place for acknowledging and responding to their feedback.

Let's get started on our way toward putting these principles in action by figuring out how to use your brand personality to extend a warm welcome for the most important asset, aside from product, that your business has—your audience.

THE WELCOME MAT

In every house I've lived in, there's always been a welcome mat outside my front door. Prior to writing this book, I couldn't have told you why except for the feeling that when I didn't have one, my house just didn't seem complete. Your brand personality is ready and waiting to chat up your audience, provide relief from what irks them, and be that friend they want and need, so why not greet your audience at the door and let them know it's okay to come inside? We need to put out the welcome mat and make this little unpopular house we're building a real home.

No matter how you do it, your brand's welcome mat should say, "Hey! We understand you, we're here, and we hear you! Come on inside, and we'll take care of you." This can be accomplished via social media presences, in-store signage, employee demeanor, or a combination of all of these and more. However you decide to send the message, it needs to show your audience that you're present and accounted for, in places where they can find you, waiting to hear what they have to say.

Putting out the welcome mat simply translates to giving your audience permission to share their thoughts because we're a culture that has become accustomed to being heard. And we don't share stuff (well, stuff worth repeating) with jerks. We share stuff with people who are locatable and easy to talk to.

Once your audience has stepped in for a spell, you've got the chance to charm them, to talk about their needs. You get to tell them your story.

SO WHAT'S *YOUR* STORY?

Your story needs to tell your audience the following:

- Who you are
- Why you're different
- Why (certain) people should care

As you craft your story using that basic list, you'll find out in short order if you sound too much like brands already in your industry. It's a fun pen-and-paper exercise and even more fun when there are two or three of you in the room answering those three questions. Try it. You'll find that a few themes keep bubbling to the surface, and you can choose the best of the best to build your brand's story.

THE CAMPFIRE CONCEPT

Unpopular brands have stories that bring the right people closer to their brand. They aren't sentences that end with periods: they end with a tempting ellipsis (. . .), inviting those who hear the story to dive in. When people hear the story, they'll say, "Yeah, that's me!" or "That's funny—I can soooo relate!" or "I hate that, too!" Great stories let your audience identify with what you've built and the value they bring to their lives. They place your audience at the center of attention. I call it the Campfire Concept.

Every brand wants to get someone's attention, and many brands think that the best way to do that is by grabbing a megaphone and yelling at anyone who will listen. But there's a better way to not only develop your brand's story but also bring the audience you want into your fold . . . and keep them there for the long haul.

People gather around a campfire because it's warm and inviting. The fire is the center of attention. When you begin telling your story, your brand is the fire and those who need to be warmed and cheered in the particular way your brand has to offer will draw near. It's warm and inviting, right?

Once that campfire audience comes to understand the brand story and see how it applies to not only their lives but also the roles they play in it, suddenly *they* become the fire—the brand exists within them. Now, *they* tell stories, share *their* brand experience, and most important, share how this brand makes their lives better. They feel included. They're a part of something. They burn with your message because it's a part of them, not something being forced on them by an external force.

When your audience becomes your fire, you've hit it out of the park. It's a fire that will continue to blaze steadily, even when your company's looking at leaner and tougher times.

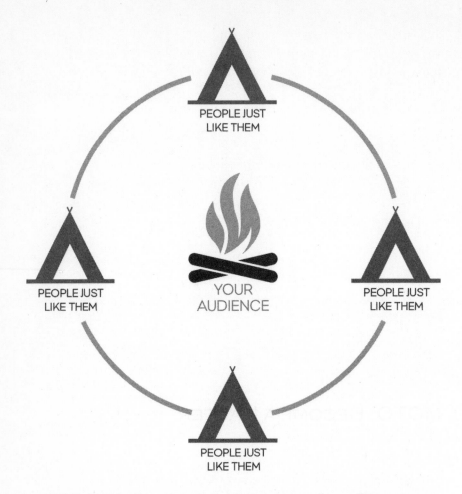

And that's why your brand needs a story: so the audience can see where you fit into their lives (and where they fit in yours). If you're a start-up looking for capital and/or press coverage, your brand story will be a vital tool in those processes as well. If you can bring potential investors and the media to the point where they feel like they are the fire, it'll be pretty hard for them to *not* want to share what you're doing. Your brand story also helps you elevate your audience, letting them know that *they* are the fundamental reason for your brand's being.

ELEVATING YOUR AUDIENCE

It's not hard to lose track of your audience when you're working every hour of the day to build a new business. At some point, we've all lost sight of the customer in pursuit of the end goal, and as a result, we've probably had some completely avoidable snafus added to our track records. From buzzwords to bullshit, we can fall so much in love with our own message that we forget that the only message we should be delivering is:

- You are my audience.
- I am grateful you give me the time of day.
- If you've got something to say, I'm ready and waiting to hear it.
- THANK YOU in advance for anything you have to share, because you're the reason I can build a brand to better serve you.

It's that simple.

Your personality invites people to your door, and putting out the welcome mat lets them know you encourage them to come inside—and on their own terms. So, what can you do to make sure audiences who have seen themselves as part of your brand story feel comfortable with *and* important enough to the brand to grab a seat and stay awhile?

MOTO: BECOME A MASTER OF THE OBVIOUS

Ever landed on a website where you can't find a contact form, phone number, or e-mail address to save your life? If your customers have to spend valuable time clicking around to find something that should be completely obvious, you're shutting them out after they've already said that they want to come inside! Unpopular, approachable brands become masters of the obvious by showing their audience that they have so much respect for their presence that they're not going to waste their time, as there is nothing more disrespectful to your audience than wasting their time. Make it *easy* for them to start a conversation, because if you don't, not only will your audience bash you for making it hard, they'll go elsewhere and start conversations with brands that haven't made communication something that requires an act of Congress to initiate.

If you have a website, make sure it's completely clear (in multiple ways) how to contact you on every page your visitors click. If you're a brick-and-mortar business, have posted in a highly visible location on your premises all the different ways people can plug into your brand and start a conversation. Let's talk for a minute about "multiple ways" to reach out to your brand.

People live in so many places online these days that we can't assume what their preferences are. If you offer only an e-mail address and someone has an urgent inquiry (maybe the media or investors trying to reach you?), you're going to find yourself missing out on opportunities, which is why I advocate offering multiple avenues for contact. Let your audience communicate with you on *their* terms. Maybe it's through Facebook, LinkedIn, or Twitter. They might prefer to leave a blog comment. Maybe they want to use your website contact form. They might be phone people, so let them make a call—and have a human being answer the phone, for all that's holy! Use a collaborative feedback platform like to the ones we'll discuss at the end of this chapter. The point is, approachable brands extend the welcome mat in multiple ways and let their audience decide how they'll initiate a conversation. By understanding your audience, you'll have a better understanding of how they prefer to communicate so that you can refine your contact options and not need to pay attention to 83 different outlets gathering feedback.

And whenever those comments, critiques, and conversations start coming in, you need to establish procedures for acknowledging and then responding to them.

We Hear You, and We're On It!

> *"Other than our brew recipe or maybe the dollar amount of one of our investor's investments, there isn't much we won't talk about in public. When people ask questions, we answer. You can see those conversations happen in public and that transparency is huge for us. We can see how much our audience appreciates it because they keep asking—and we will keep answering."*
>
> —Mark Hellendrung, CEO, Narragansett Beer

A key component to being an approachable brand comes from how you participate in conversations with your audience. Having all these nifty contact forms on your website and fancy feedback tools isn't going to do you a damn bit of good if you're not respecting your audience enough to acknowledge and respond.

It's about respect—if you've put your brand out there as being friendly, opened the door, and told your audience it's okay to come inside and start a conversation, it's pretty bunk to not respect them enough to acknowledge that they're sitting right there in your living room. So, to bear in mind:

- **If you build it, maintain it.** A fair amount of my consulting work is devoted to either building new social presences and strategies or evaluating existing ones. Many companies have tried the strategy of setting up a gazillion social media profiles and then end up leaving them to wither and die in the marketplace sun. You can't do that. If you set something up, it requires proper care and feeding. Put another way, it requires interaction—from *you*. If you have a customer who is an avid Facebook user, and that person leaves a comment on your page that goes ignored for three weeks, you've lied about being approachable. This goes for any presence you establish for your company, from phone lines (again—*humans* answer phones; *computers* do not) to contact forms to online social profiles.

- **Have reasonable response times.** Truly approachable brands respect their audience enough to respond to inquiries, questions, comments, and social feedback in a reasonable amount of time. The coolest part of this is that any contact from your audience is a new opportunity to gain trust and demonstrate how approachable you are. Customers tend to place more trust in brands where they can see them responding to questions, offering thanks, and resolving issues in the public eye than in those who may or may not be handling issues. How are we supposed to know what a brand does or thinks if we can't see the evidence?

- **Know the value of mea culpa.** Again, brands are whos. They're human. They make mistakes. Being approachable as a brand means being willing to hear from your target audience across the entire scope of sentiment. If you royally screw the pooch, you have to be willing to not only respond to but also resolve the situation with grace. (In cases of pooch screwing, a mea culpa is a must.) Be open and honest about the screwup, ask for forgiveness, explain your solution, and let the world know that you own it. Think for a moment about the brand missteps you've heard about in the past 12 to 24 months. There's generally more focus on how the brand handled the incident than on the incident itself.

- **Make the ask.** Be sure you're asking your audience to come through the front door by clearly demonstrating all of the options available to contact you. It's such a pain to have to hunt around for "back door" solutions by digging through a website's site map or using web searches. Some people are more hesitant to reach out than others and need to see more than just the option to contact you. Approachable brands explain from time to time all of the different ways you can reach out to them; they make it clear that they're interested in hearing what you have to say, as well as make it easy for you to participate in the process. Think about Facebook Questions. Surveys. Quick polls. Links to your customer service forums and FAQs shared on social networks and on in-store signs. If someone's made it through the front door, that person has expressed that he or she is open to participating. Make it easy for someone to make the leap from user to influencer.
- **Assign responsibility.** Don't leave the important obligation (and privilege) of interacting with your customers the chance to fall victim to a "I thought *you* were checking the customer service e-mail inbox/Twitter account/Facebook page." Make sure that you clearly state who has responsibility for staying on top of any outlet for customer feedback and social interaction at any given time. It might sound like a *duh,* but we've all had one of those, "I thought you were . . ." conversations in our careers. Dealing with the fallout sucks.

BRINGING APPROACHABILITY FULL CIRCLE

Product? Check.
Audience? Identified.
Personality they'll like? Building it.

Using all three to invite your audience deeper inside your brand? The task at hand.

I can say from firsthand experience that through a boatload of trial and error, I've built a brand that encourages open and honest conversation not only between my audience and me but among the audience members themselves. Few moments are more inspiring than watching your customers get to know one another, build relationships, launch banter, and use one another as resources! And there's a definite upside: you can get some of your best ideas for blog posts, stories, and new ways to take care of your clients by having an audience that's comfortable enough with your brand to bring ideas to your door. It's like having a giant news feed of ideas. When your audience sees you as approachable, you're working smarter. They bring you ideas for how to make your service or product better, or they take the time to tell you what they love so that you don't have to go out and look for that feedback. Sure, you have to maintain the outlets you've adopted to bring that feedback through the door, but maintaining those is a lot less exhausting than not having them and continually having to wonder what the hell is going through your audience's mind.

Now, with your welcome mat in place and your audience arriving to share, you may need some assistance making sense of the information you begin to receive. A couple of resources are available to brands of any size that can help in that department.

Get Satisfaction and UserVoice

You know that being approachable is fundamental to getting the feedback you need to grow and prosper. And your customers now know that they have a voice in the development of your brand. But did you know that there are brands out there completely dedicated to making that interface happen between you and your customers?

Get Satisfaction and UserVoice, both early-stage technology companies out of San Francisco, California, are in the business of helping brands do better business. They do this by bridging the gap between you and your audience and offering ways for your audience to give you feedback on a variety of issues—and in an organized fashion. Wendy Lea, chief executive officer (CEO) of Get Satisfaction, and Scott Rutherford, chief operating officer (COO) and cofounder of UserVoice, share their respective company's humble beginnings, along with how they're using their own platforms to continuously evolve their product for their audience's benefit.

ALWAYS ON—GET SATISFACTION

www.getsatisfaction.com; @GetSatisfaction

Lane Becker and Thor and Amy Muller started Ruby Red Labs, a boutique development shop in San Francisco that built web applications and sites for start-ups. They were also the founders of Valleyschwag, a company that created a secondary market for all of the branded *schwag* various companies produce for trade shows and other promotional events, such as T-shirts, hats, and tote bags. One of Valleyschwag's European customers had a problem while the company's American-based team was sleeping and posted a question on the company's blog. The Valleyschwag/Ruby Red Labs team awoke to find that multiple people had come in and given this customer the answer he was looking for.

Then they started thinking about the potential in building something that allowed that kind of collaboration and cooperation to happen, not just coincidentally but all the time.

They launched Get Satisfaction in 2007.

As of late 2011, Get Satisfaction has more than 62,000 communities seeking feedback from their respective audience bases in their network, led, moderated, and owned by employees and companies of all sizes. In that sixty-some-odd-thousand, there are 2,500 who have chosen to pay to have access to more robust feature sets on their platform—and it's only getting better. They take on anywhere between 250 and 350 new paying customers each month, along with roughly 2,000 additional free accounts.

Customer feedback is big business as well. This 40-employee company's revenue has grown 100 percent year over year, and they currently log $8 million in bookings on an annual basis. For 2012, their revenue target is aggressive: in the $20 to $25 million range. With numbers and growth like that, it's no wonder they've found a devoted set of investors in the venture capital community and have to date raised $20.1 million in paid-in capital to fuel the company's vision.

And it all began with eight people (three of whom were founders) and $500,000 in the bank.

A Bit about JarGon

When you stop by Get Satisfaction's website, you might see a little robot named JarGon in various locations. "He's our mascot," Wendy Lea shares. "We are in an epic battle with Jargon. We encourage our companies to be honest, open and communicate with an authentic tone. Buzzspeak and jargon don't encourage trust and collaboration." They've come up with a pretty fun way to get that message across. Robots don't speak like people—and the brands that can learn to speak to their audience in approachable and understandable language are the ones that find themselves pulling ahead of the pack.

Behind the Growth

So, how was this company founded in 2007 aiming for the high side of $25 million in revenues only five short years later? "We're an open network of communities which gives a space for companies and customers to ask questions, solve problems, share ideas and give praise—honestly and easily (similar to what would happen in the hotel lobby of a high-end hotel). Because the network is open, those conversations are being searched by Google, creating an opportunity for the conversations to be highly discoverable by other customers with similar questions. The search engine optimization (SEO) benefit we provide to customers in our network is significant," explains Wendy. "Most customers use Google as their starting place for questions and problems. Oftentimes the customer is taken directly to a thread inside the Get Satisfaction community as a result of this SEO benefit."

Search engine optimization (SEO) is a practice whereby web developers make sure that the search engines can find your website and offer it as a relevant result when people search the Internet for what your company has to offer. For example, if your company sells ground coffee in Peoria, Illinois, proper SEO helps the search engines understand that someone searching for a company that sells ground coffee in Peoria and/or Illinois should be offered your company as a search result.

As a result, the company has never had to do any traditional marketing—SEO and word-of-mouth referrals together have ensured that. However, that doesn't mean they've gotten to where they are without give and take. Wendy explains the company's "always-on" philosophy.

> Given how our product is built, companies can determine who receives the suggestions their users submit. [We know that] we have an obligation to use our product to its maximum—and we think the best way to do that at present is for our management and development team to be exposed to everything. There's a good reason for that, especially as a company that's developing, marketing, and continuously seeking to improve a customer and user feedback platform.
>
> The social web's pretty much guaranteed that we—our company and customers alike—operate in an always-on, real-time feedback world. If you've got an Internet connection, you have a voice. We owe it to our customers to be in that same "always-on" position. At first, I'll admit that I felt like freaking out seeing all the feedback notifications in my inbox each morning. It's easy to feel continuously criticized and judged. When you step back though, it doesn't take long to shift from feeling as if you've been attacked to understanding you've just been armed with the most valuable information possible—and from the people that want what you have to offer. What more could you ask for than open, honest customers providing feedback?
>
> We are the ones who can immediately take our customers' expressions and determine what we can use in varying degrees of right now to raise the level of satisfaction and loyalty to our brand. We've grown because we listen. I never want to wake up each morning and not have that flow of feedback and suggestions waiting for me in my inbox. It's the best kind of wake-up call!

It was those suggestions waiting in Wendy's inbox each morning that told her their customers wanted to be able to use Get Satisfaction's capabilities to build feedback communities directly from their brand's Facebook fan pages. With the vast number of requests for that type of functionality, she knew it had to be prioritized—yet there was a hitch: "At the time, we had five developers who were working full-time on our company's needs and not a whole lot of money to go out and hire more. On top of that, we weren't a company with Facebook expertise. If we were going to make this happen, I needed to go out and find a partner to help us deliver this solution."

Yet out of their limited resources, they were still able to grow. Wendy found Involver (www.involver.com), a company that specializes in developing apps that enhance the user experience for Facebook fan pages. It turned out to be the ideal relationship, and in 2010, Get Satisfaction announced full Facebook integration. At present, more than 1,000 of their customers are using this functionality to better engage customers by building communities from their fan pages.

Quid Pro Quo—Exchanging Information with Their Audience (Education)

Get Satisfaction isn't just a brand that uses its own platform to build a better product. They're also one that believes in a quid pro quo with its audience. "Our audience is gracious enough to share their thoughts with us, so we do the same for them in return on a regular basis," Wendy says. They do this though weekly webcasts and newsletters, which are their opportunity to give back to the customers who help improve their product. They feature everything from customer success stories to training on new features they've brought online to best practices around community management—anything that can help their customers use their product to its highest possible level to improve their businesses. The webcasts and additional newsletters that they send out aren't sales-y in nature—just a solid library of resources that let customers know that Get Satisfaction is listening and invested in their customers' success beyond what their product can offer.

Takeaway Tips for Any Business: Processing Time, Walking Away, and Owning Your Role

Although Get Satisfaction is a relative newcomer to the customer relationship management (CRM) space, Wendy Lea isn't. She's had an interesting line to walk, to say the least, since joining the company in 2009. As a veteran of CRM (people, process, and technology), yet a newcomer to the world of online businesses and social feedback, she has these tips for any business that's looking to make better decisions with a little (or a lot) of help from its customers.

- **Jumping to Conclusions:** Customer feedback is a powerful thing, but if you're not careful, you're going to feel like you're in a weird remake of *Office Space* marketing a Jump to Conclusions mat. When you get feedback, take the time to clarify and probe further. It's easy to look at a single piece and then prematurely run with it, but there's the potential to trip and fall. Oftentimes (and fess up—you know it's happened before), we think we're responding to something when we're really not. And it's all because we didn't take an extra step or two to understand the situation behind the information. Listen and understand before you commit and act.
- **Finding the Value in Pondering:** No one's advocating that you take an extended European vacation, but when you've reached a point of understanding this feedback you asked for—context and all—sit on it for a sec, would ya? Companies poised for growth rarely have the luxury of making leisurely business decisions, but you can take the time to vet the problem and the proposed solution. This adds an entirely different dimension. Test and iterate.
- **Understanding Your Goals:** Just like any brand on the rise, Get Satisfaction built its product for users who were looking for an open and honest platform to gather feedback from their audience. Occasionally, there's a prospective customer who comes along wanting the product to be something it's not. And that's where understanding your goals comes in.

Just as Get Satisfaction doesn't implement every piece of advice that their users submit as recommendations, no company should bend to appease every customer that walks through the door. It's a matter of responsibility and integrity for both your audience and your brand. The onus is on you to share with your audience your company's direction and culture, as well a how the audience's ideas fit (or don't) into where the brand is headed.

Brands of all shapes and sizes are using Get Satisfaction, from giants like Proctor & Gamble and Walmart to the savviest Silicon Valley start-ups like Flipboard and StumbleUpon. When you're looking for a way to make your audience a part of the ongoing solution for your brand, check them out. They'll help you find a way to be "always on" for your audience—no matter what your budget is—*and* they'll help you skip bringing JarGon on as a full-time staffer in the process.

COOKING (AND EATING) YOUR OWN DOG FOOD—USERVOICE

www.uservoice.com; @UserVoice

In 2008, you would have found UserVoice founders Richard White and Scott Rutherford in a one-room granny flat out behind a bungalow occupied by their third founder, Marcus, in Santa Cruz, California. They spent their days coding, and their nights ended when they fell asleep on their computers. If you consider two guys living in a one-room apartment to be glamorous, sure—there was glamour at UserVoice. However, they've built a business around solving a very unglamorous problem: turning data into information.

Both founders had experienced the personal pain of launching products online and then having their respective inboxes explode with e-mails full of feature requests and bug reports. Data. And it was a tiring and inefficient process dealing with it, to say the least. They knew there had to be a better way to not only organize this influx of data but also prioritize it so that the most important tasks floated to the top. In English, that translated to:

- What type of request is it? (feature, bug report, user interface, etc.)
- Who else wants it?
- How important is it to the product?
- When should we as a company implement it?

They began, as most start-ups do, with a minimally viable product, and in 2009 they landed their first round of funding. At the time, they had roughly a couple-hundred dollars in monthly revenue coming in and 5,000 different companies using their platform.

Today, in excess of 23 million people have come through the UserVoice system and shared their feedback with the more than 73,000 companies using the platform. Annual revenue is in the low millions. And the kicker? They built UserVoice using UserVoice, a process that Scott Rutherford calls "cooking and eating your own dog food," and they've been doing it from day one.

How UserVoice Used UserVoice to Shape Their Product

"We're a very real company and put honesty and transparency out there as our core principles," says Scott. "We've built a team that not only lives and breathes our product, but that believes that there's a better way to do things." It's a concept that's worked well, especially since UserVoice's product focuses on getting their customers' feedback from the people who can offer the best insight: their users. So how has UserVoice tapped their product and learned from it in the process?

GUIDES FOR PRICING

UserVoice operates on a "freemium" model, which means their basic services are free and additional features come under different pricing plans. As they were developing their revenue model, they would actively ask their users if they would pay X for X or if they charged X, what their audience would want for that expenditure. The result was that their users essentially developed their pricing structure. "When you have 400 people who have just said that they'd pay X dollars for X service, you've got your price. You take that feedback and put it into action," says Rutherford. They posted a link to the new plan in that conversation thread, and the people who asked for it came over and signed up.

Product Direction—The Ability to Say No (and for a Good Reason)

UserVoice operates on an upvote system, which means users of a product who are interested in a certain feature give it a ranking from 1 to 3 points. Each user is given 10 points to spend, so it helps eliminate the potential for overpowering influence from heavy users (people who spend a lot of time in the system). But can you downvote something you don't like? Nope. Scott explains why:

> Everyone's happy to say, "Yeah—that's a great idea," but who's comfortable, especially from a product standpoint, telling their customers no? We opted to not include downvotes as an option because it [encourages] a battle between users instead of focusing on things you're actually interested in. Why not spend time trying to get something implemented instead of actively trying to kill it? The upvotes are a more constructive sentiment and pretty much take gaming out of the equation since it's easier to bury an idea than it is to get it voted up.

Through the upvote system, UserVoice users widely upvoted a certain product development—and then UserVoice came in and said no. Scott explained that this particular scenario made them recognize the value in their platform for shaping the direction of their business. Although the requested feature had overwhelming appeal with their users, it wasn't in line with where the company's direction was headed. So how did they deal with telling their customers no? Anytime a client rejects a feature, they are required to provide an explanation to their users as to why. So UserVoice told UserVoice users (that's a mouthful, isn't it?) why the feature wouldn't be added and explained some things about where they were headed with their product. It was a key combination of not only being accessible to your audience and thanking them for being part of the solution but also acknowledging that they had helped the UserVoice team crystallize more completely where they saw their company heading.

Prioritization and What Makes Brands Better

One of the biggest challenges we all face as brand builders is prioritization. How do you triage everything that needs to be done against the resources you have available to get them completed? The UserVoice team found that their audience was the best way to tell them what needed to be done versus what needed to be done now. From Facebook integration to localization (their platform is currently available in 42 languages and counting), these things wouldn't have made it to the top of the priority list without not only the insistence of their audience but also a way to organize that feedback so that they could act on it as quickly as possible.

The upvote system allows brands to track both interest in certain features and improvements and also the speed at which they are upvoted. And, through their own prioritization process, they noticed that most of the recommendations being made weren't necessarily what would be considered big changes. They were small steps. "They're the things that help clients provide a richer user experience—things you don't think about because you're not in there using it every day, and you're too close to the product," Scott explains. "They're the things about a product that make it a better place to be. You've done the heavy lifting with your product and brand, getting it 80 to 85 percent of where it needs to be. These small things? That's the audience taking you the other 15 to 20 percent of the way."

Takeaway Tips from a User Feedback Company to Brands Looking for User Feedback

"Lack of success due to inactivity is the worst failure ever," states Scott. The least effective thing you can do for a product or brand is to do absolutely nothing. Scott was kind enough to share some of the best practices they've seen for creating a culture that lets their audience know their thoughts are valued so that they can carry that approachability through their entire brand and product development process.

- **Understand your business development cycle:** Although technology companies are used to hearing the terms *alpha* and *beta* phases, you might not be.
  - *Alphas* are generally what are considered minimally viable product, or merely functioning versions of what you'd like to build so that people can start (quietly) using it and giving you feedback.

○ *Betas* are more developed versions of your product, but definitely not the finished iteration. Betas are generally offered to a wider audience than an alpha product release.

During these early stages, you want to tap into early adopters—an audience who will be anxious to test and offer suggestions on how to improve what you're building. They're interested in helping you move your product forward and tend to be very tolerant of bugs and early-stage challenges to your product.

For the first six months, you're going to be figuring out your product–market fit—in other words, how your product more fully addresses the needs of the audience you're building it for and how you need to get that ship tightened up to move it along. Embrace that beginning stage where your active and willing audience will tell you what works, what doesn't, and how they'd like to see your product and brand come to fruition.

- **Don't build in a vacuum:** Remember when Scott said that failure due to inactivity was a huge miss? Building a product in a vacuum is essentially the same as doing nothing. You have to get your brand and its moving parts into the hands of the people you're building it for. Scott calls this process "iterating among the people." When you allow your target audience in from the beginning, they can cluster around concepts and you can discuss how they'd like to see their suggestions implemented, as well as what's a priority. It's the standard case of failure to launch. If you're too afraid to put a product out there, you're never going to get the feedback you need from the audience you want to allow you to go forth and kick ass. You're really just kicking your own ass.

So who's using UserVoice? The names vary from local community projects across the world to major names across every possible industry, including Rackspace, Stack Overflow, Teach for America, the City of Vancouver, MTV, Deloitte, and more each day. Check them out on the web and never be afraid to tell them how they're doing. They're listening.

PUTTING APPROACHABILITY IN PERSPECTIVE

The process of honoring your audience and ensuring they know you've put out the welcome mat is one that you'll find to be never ending as you travel your brand-building path. Being unpopular isn't about shutting people out; it's about continuously finding ways to encourage the *right* people to come inside. Approachable brands aren't above their audience—they're on par with them. If your audience is going to be persuaded to come in and try to be a collaborative partner, your brand needs a personality and a set of practices that makes them feel comfortable.

On that note, let's head to Lawrenceville, New Jersey, and discover how a plumbing supply company founded in 1935 can help you build better relationships with your audience and use those relationships to compete with your industry's behemoths. Offering the welcome mat is a state of mind and just as much a component of your brand's overall texture as anything else.

And Mrs. G is one lady who had that down to a science.

CASE IN POINT: MRS. G'S TV & APPLIANCES

HOW A NEW JERSEY ONE-OFF IS ALWAYS ON

You'd never guess upon walking into Mrs. G's 20,000-square-foot showroom that they started out as a plumbing supply company. Back in 1935, Abe and Beatrice Greenberg opened New Jersey Plumbing in Trenton, New Jersey, selling plumbing supplies to the local community. At the end of World War II, the business community they called home experienced a tremendous change—there was a family surge. Servicemen returning from the war were starting families left and right, and those families needed the latest household appliances. And that's when the Greenbergs started selling refrigerators, stoves, and the like. It's also when they realized that there was more to building a successful business than just offering appliances.

In the company's formative days, customers could walk into the store and see Beatrice each and every day. She was the face of the store, talking to customers and their children and getting to know the people who were keeping New Jersey Plumbing's doors open day after day. If a family needed a new stove or refrigerator and couldn't afford the entire purchase price, they were sent to see Mrs. G. She'd sit and talk to the customer about everything from their family, work, and needs, and chances were that if she were satisfied with what she heard, that family would walk out with a refrigerator on a $5-per-week payment plan. It was simple: know your customers who know your business and find a way to meet them in the middle.

Eventually, New Jersey Plumbing would relocate to Ewing and finally to its current home in Lawrenceville. It would also undergo a name change, becoming "Mrs. G's," a tribute to the cofounder who never had an office, was always on the showroom floor, and was willing to go the extra mile to help customers by being the most approachable person in the store and, arguably, their community.

And They Remain Family Owned, in One Location

Although Mrs. G's represents the humble beginnings familiar to many businesses, their brand also poses the paradoxical question about how a local business can compete in a landscape (seemingly) dominated by big-box behemoths. That's a question I asked Debbie Schaeffer, Beatrice's granddaughter and present CEO of Mrs. G's:

> Since my grandmother grew up in the Depression, she always considered the store's pricing model to be "discount pricing." But that changed when Home Depot and Lowe's came in. They came into the area full-force, opening six stores within a ten-mile delivery radius, putting a fair amount of pressure on the business.

(continued)

(*continued*)

We saw the big-box retailers competing with us on price—commoditizing the appliance market in our community. We were faced with two decisions: jump into the price war or offer something that took pricing out of the equation. We opted for the latter and moved into high-end appliance lines like Sub-Zero, Wolf, Viking, Thermador, and Miele. As a result of our move, we attracted business that they weren't even targeting, yet we were sneaky. We were still able to compete on price because of how we built our business and structured our buying practices.

We're a part of the largest buying and marketing organization in the country called Nationwide Marketing Group. It's a group of over 3,000 locally owned retailers and independents just like Mrs. G's, operating a combined total of 8,000 store fronts, who together create in excess of $12 billion in buying power. A smaller business just starting out might think that they can't compete on price alone. While that's true, a combination of a smart business model mixed with buying groups specific to your industry can level the playing field when the big boys move in. As a result, we've built a business that serves a niche our perceived competitors can't, and because of our buying power, we can continue to offer a price matching policy, great sales, and in many cases, not discount at all because our floor price is already lower than their sale price. [The bigger stores would have to play] a huge game of catch-up to even begin to gain ground. And that's where our approachable business model has proven invaluable.

Talk to Us. Please.

From the day my grandmother opened this business, she never had an office—and I don't have one, either. My office is a reception desk located right by the front door. My grandmother was always out there talking to our customers, and as a result, our customers knew they could always talk to her. She could also see everything going on across the sales floor, and that's something I enjoy very much as well. We chose to work *in* our business. People are always surprised when I answer the main phone line coming into the store, and I just think, "Why?" I don't really know the business model of building something up so you can spend as little time in it as possible. I'm always ready to answer the phone, talk to a customer, follow up on an order. This is how you build relationships, and we wouldn't be anywhere without the trusted relationships we've built over the years.

When you try building a business where there's no ongoing conversation with your customers, you're passing up an incredibly valuable opportunity. Why would you turn off a channel on the television where you had a constant influx of people who were ready to tell you what they love, what needs improving, and how your business can better serve their needs? We keep that channel turned on, and not just because we sell TVs! We keep it on because they allow us to keep it on, and in return, we show the community that we appreciate their input by being a part of it beyond the doors of our store.

Our Customers, Our Community

While we still follow some more traditional paths for getting our brand out there like ads in local papers, radio, and magazines, we've added a significant community involvement component to the business. Here are two examples where we show our customers that we're invested in the community, as well as the generations that have supported our business and will continue to—past, present, and future.

(continued)

(*continued*)

- **Sponsoring Local Sports Teams:** We proudly sponsor the Class AA Affiliate of the New York Yankees, Trenton Thunder baseball team located in Trenton, New Jersey. We sponsor a game mini-plan where we give away six appliances throughout the course of the season. At each game, we have a table set up with the appliance giveaway and up to 5,000 ticket holders at each game visit our table to sign up for a chance to win the giveaway. What do we get by giving things away? The community sees us at every game while they're doing something they love, and we get to be a part of that fun.

- **Charitable Giving:** We make it a point to help out with as many school and charitable groups each year as our budget will allow. These families are our current customers, their parents were probably customers, and we have no intention of going anywhere so we hope to earn their children as customers as well. If our donations can help a school get better books or fund programs that give our community's children a richer educational experience, we're all about that. And above all—people in the community know they can ask us for these donations and that we welcome their requests.

So how do we see all of these efforts coming back to us? Our most recent tent sale had a fabulous turnout across the entire community. We've built a business that's way beyond price shopping, as over half of the inventory sold during that sale wasn't from the tents, but from our showroom floor. People know we support the community, and when they come to our store, it's about the experience and relationship. Yes, we have the largest Sub-Zero/Wolf living kitchen in the country and over eight live displays where people can do anything from cook a meal to do their laundry. When we ask our new customers how they heard of Mrs. G's, the most common answer is: their parents, friends, neighbor, realtor, designer, architect, or contractor. A customer referral is the most effective form of marketing. And that is the secret to our success. We understand how our community lives and that's what drives our marketing decisions each and every day.

Strategies to Emulate

Although it's a fact that there are few people reading this book who are going to rush out and open an appliance business, Debbie's insight on why they built Mrs. G's the way they did is invaluable in many ways. Not only does it demonstrate that you don't have to be a behemoth to best serve your target audience, it's a great example of why competing on price alone is a B.S. strategy.

So what are some of the other things Mrs. G's is doing that your business can emulate?

On Social Media

Mrs. G's latched on to a social strategy pretty early on and, as a result, gained a respectable amount of local traction through their online presences. They first started on Twitter because not only could they share information about their business and sales, they could also help promote things in the local community. They then chose to pursue Facebook and LinkedIn and saw the biggest benefit to these outlets to be the improvement in their search engine results from having profiles on these different sites. They continue to use them day in and day out, and Debbie even met her publicist, Hilary Morris, through a local Tweetup, which is a gathering of people in a community organized through Twitter. Not having been too familiar with social media prior to this Tweetup, she was surprised when she walked in and before even introducing herself, people knew who she was. That alone started multiple conversations and was a powerful way for her to deepen her company's involvement in the community.

(continued)

(*continued*)

The Merger of Social and Physical

When Debbie met Hilary through that local Tweetup event, they started a conversation about how they could give back to the social community that introduced them. The area was rich with bloggers and other people who were highly active in social media circles, and although they couldn't go the route of auto-maker heavyweight Ford who was giving bloggers a car, they did come up with a strategy that proved to be more than they'd ever hoped. They created Mrs. G's VIBs (very important bloggers) and hosted a yearlong lunch-and-learn series for this highly targeted audience. The topics ranged from new 3D television technology to how to prepare a healthy meal for the family. Not only did Mrs. G's get new people in the door, but they developed a loyal group of people who not only were happy to write about their experience in the store but referred their online followers to do business with her—and look to Mrs. G's for future events and partnerships with a social media focus.

Takeaway Tips for Any Business

Mrs. G's has created a legacy as an approachable brand since Abe and Beatrice Greenberg went into business back in 1935. Although your business might not be more than 70 years old, what you can glean from their example is that building an approachable brand is more than about having a contact form on your website or just replying when people ask you a question. It's about putting yourself where your customers live, finding out what's important to them and your community, and making those things your business's priority as well.

- **Be *in* your business.** Whether you have a brick-and-mortar location with a showroom or you're working out of a home office, you have to be present. If you're not there to interact with your customers, who is speaking on your behalf? This is a full-time job, especially as your business is getting its sea legs and even more so when you're going through growth phases. It doesn't mean you can't take time off like any other normal human being. It means don't confuse owning a business with being on a full-time vacation and a part-time work schedule. It's definitely the other way around.

- **Let people know that you care about the business and its customers.** There are so many ways you can do this, from being present in your business to asking for feedback and responding—even when that feedback comes unsolicited. The point is, your customers will determine whether your doors stay open. When you take the time to be active in their lives, understand what's important to them, and give back to the community where you all live, you're putting yourself and your business in a position to not just be a business that sells to your community but one that also serves it.

- **Are you on Facebook?** If you have a consumer-facing business with a brick-and-mortar location, you should be on Facebook. Mrs. G's adopted the platform early on, but know today that if they hadn't, it would have been harder to gain traction there if they had waited. If you want to keep your business growing across generations, you have to figure out what those generations are doing. And this generation? Well, it's on Facebook. Mrs. G's is learning more and more about how to use the platform each day.

- **Never bad-mouth your competitors.** Honestly, it's just poor form. More businesses should remember that they're able to grow and succeed because of things their competitors do and don't do, so embrace them and make a commitment to overserve and never underappreciate your customers and community. Bad-mouthing just makes you look petty and does nothing to let your audience know that you're savvy, interested in their needs, and looking to be an integral part of the community you seek to serve.

(continued)

(continued)

If you have doubts about making yourself accessible to your community, this last bit from Debbie might seal the deal for you:

> The day after my grandmother's funeral, I was at the corner pizza parlor by my daughter's school in Pennington. The owner, whom I'd never met, came up to me and told me that he'd heard about my grandmother's passing and extended his condolences. He also said when he emigrated from Italy, Mrs. G was the only one who would give him credit on a new appliance. That alone allowed him to open the doors on the business I was standing in that day.

Mrs. G's TV & Appliances
Lawrenceville, New Jersey
Website: www.mrsgs.com
Facebook: www.facebook.com/MrsGsNJ
Twitter: @Mrs_Gs

CHAPTER 5

SHARABILITY

GETTING YOUR AUDIENCE TO THE ROOFTOPS (AND LETTING THEM SHOUT)

In the second season of *Mad Men*, the persistent Peggy is left in charge of pitching Popsicle when Don Draper, creative director for the fictional Sterling Cooper ad agency, goes MIA. The client apparently wants to sell more frozen treats, even when the weather goes frosty—so how do they get past the fact that Popsicles have been perceived as a warm-weather treat?

In a wave of nostalgia, Peggy remembers that her mother would buy the treats from the ice cream truck, break them in half (they were twin pops, the Siamese twins of frozen confections), and give one to her and one to her sister. They were always shared. As soon as she voiced her musing out loud, a fellow Sterling Cooperite concurred; it was the same in his house, too.

Audiences tuned in to Peggy leading a pitch meeting featuring the new ad slogan, "Take it, break it, share it, love it." It's what people had been doing with Popsicles all along, so they created a weather-resistant campaign that took product seasonality off the table. Sharing, they realized, is something that could be done year-round.

And it's a fundamental part of any unpopular brand.

ROOFTOPS (AND WHY WE LOVE THEM)

What's the first thing we do when we find something we can't live without? We shout our praise from the rooftops. There's a fever that boils up inside, making it impossible to *not* share with everyone we know this thing we've discovered. When you're building the un-popular brand, you should be aiming for the rooftops, giving your audience both the reasons and the means to share you with everyone they know.

But why do we share? We could be greedy little bastards and keep all of the good stuff for ourselves, but that's not how you win friends and gain influence, is it? Sharing is driven by a few motivations.

- **Altruism:** We want to do what we can to help the causes and people we care about. If they have a message we support, we want to share that message and help them reach their goals.
- **Authority:** Can we admit that we all want that little rush that comes from being the person who told so-and-so about such-and-such? Think back to brand personality and the friends you

have who are go-tos for certain things. We trust them and want them to trust us as well. We earn that go-to status by sharing things we trust with the people we trust.

- **Community:** Sharing makes us a part of something bigger than ourselves. We want (and need) to belong and be a part of a story, and sharing the tribe's message identifies us as belonging with the community. It helps build relationships.

On our journey toward unpopular so far, we've taken the guess-work out of audience identification and determined some solid ways for figuring out who's already asking for what we're building. A brand story well told (the Campfire Concept) will help those people feel included, making them willing to step up to your front door. Then it's up to you to invite them inside and make them feel not only welcome but also indispensable.

RECRUITING YOUR BRAND ADVOCATE ARMY

During World War II, the U.S. military demands were so high that factories found themselves with a shortage of labor—labor that was necessary to keep our armed forces properly outfitted for the war in Europe. The solution? They turned to a resource they'd never used prior to that point: women. Before World War II, women were a minority influence in the U.S. workforce, but between 1940 and 1944, the number of women in the workforce increased nearly 57 percent, to 20 million—and all because industrial society sent out three very important messages:

- We want you.
- We need you.
- Please show your support by joining the workforce—you're indispensable.

Indispensable to an Allied victory. To what it meant to be an American. To the future of the country. To their families. They were needed and desired, and in an entirely new way by something much larger than themselves.

In the twenty-first century, we can apply the iconic Rosie the Riveter to what every unpopular brand needs to do: recruit a Brand Advocate Army.

At the beginning of Chapter 4, we discussed how marketing has undergone a shift from outbound, one-way messages to primarily collaborative inbound efforts. Referrals and recommendations are a primary reason that business even has the opportunity to get done in today's society. Your brand's personality and approachability give you the opportunity to establish the kind of relationship with your audience that makes them not only love you but also want to share you with everyone they know. And although Brand Advocate Army may sound corny, we have to call it something. Why not go with a full-on dose of corny so we can share a smile when we think about our audience with the affection they deserve?

WHY YOU NEED A BRAND ADVOCATE ARMY

Your brand's audience is its single most powerful marketing tool, so there's no better use of your time and marketing dollars than the cultivating of long-term relationships with your audience. You'll build your Brand Advocate Army by nurturing your audience over time, making them feel so well taken care of that they're compelled to get up on those rooftops and start shouting your brand message to everyone they know. Here's why that's important:

- **Trust:** We're more likely to trust recommendations from people we know. This leads to . . .
- **Lower Barriers to Entry:** Endorsement from a trusted resource shortens—and in many cases, even removes—the usual trust-building phase people go through when deciding to do business with a new company.
- **Targeting:** When you earn a customer and put the effort into keeping her or him, that's the most targeted marketing resource you could ever design. These customers love your product, know *their* audience, and will share you with people that *they* know will love you.

AND SO WE BUILD—THE FUNDAMENTALS OF SHARABILITY

We're back to the lists as we take a look at the four factors that will encourage people to share your brand.

- **Altruism (humans want to help):** Job number 1 of any unpopular brand—we talked about this in "rooftops."
- **Trust (being seen as an authority):** Giving your audience reasons to send people your way (and removing the reasons that keep people away).
- **The Beauty of Off-Topic Conversation (it's the glue that keeps communities together):** Because humans aren't one-trick ponies.
- **Tools:** There is a wide range of tools available to help you encourage your audience to share your brand, as well as set the metrics to better understand how this very sharing affects it. Make it easy to share and understand where and how you're being shared.

Building the ladder that will get people to those rooftops starts with taking an altruistic approach to your audience.

GET OVER YOURSELF

Remember That Guy? It's impossible to build a sharable brand when you're That Guy, because he's not interested in anything except himself. That Guy kind of brands are the ones that are on topic, all the time, and see marketing as all about *me me me*. Unpopular brands are the opposite of egocentric; they're entirely altruistic in nature. To be sharable, the first thing you have to do is get over yourself and embrace that 80 percent of your messaging should be about everything *except* your brand.

Yup, you read that right: only 20 percent of what you put out into the business ether should be about your company, your products, your announcements, and anything else that happens inside of your brand walls. Nobody wants to sit down with That Guy for very long, because there's nothing interesting about talking about him 24/7. When you've taken the time to get to know your audience, determine where they hang out, learn what's important to them, and how your solution adds value to that equation, it works best if you put your solution right where I did on the list: last. You have to talk to your audience about what matters to them—and most of the time, it sure as hell isn't your product, service, or brand.

Relationships aren't built by asking people to do things for you and pay attention to you; they're built by asking people, "What can I do for *you?*" It's the same thing when you're asking your audience to share you (your brand) with *their* trusted audience. When you take a minute to get over yourself, you can start being a brand with an altruistic perspective that asks its audience how *you* can help *them.* When you spend 80 percent of your time talking about what's important to your audience, they continue to see themselves in your brand story. Something else pretty cool happens, too: they start to build relationships with other members of your audience. Before you know it, you're on your way to building a community—that Brand Advocate Army.[1] You've cultivated a collective of people who care about your brand because you've demonstrated that you're one of them and are interested in what they find important. We'll talk even more about communities in Chapter 9.

Altruism can take many forms, but the easiest way to look at it is from the social perspective. There are plenty of ways to help your audience that have nothing at all (yet everything) to do with your product or service. Maybe you have a customer that's running a half marathon to raise money for charity. The altruistic and sharable brand shares with its audience first. It donates a day's worth of tips, posts a link on its social web presences, or writes a blog so that other members of the brand's audience know how to lend a helping hand. Insert any matter of importance to your audience into that model and determine how your business can get involved.

BEING A TRUSTED RESOURCE

Nobody goes into business with the hopes of building the crappiest [blank]. Brands that find traction understand the importance of becoming a trusted resource in their individual areas of expertise.

---

[1] If you're interested in learning more about building your Brand Advocate Army, be sure to check out *Trust Agents* by Chris Brogan and Julien Smith (Wiley, 2009).

It doesn't matter if you're a local dry cleaner or an information technology (IT) consulting firm; you want your audience to trust that you are the best at what you do and feel confident that they can rely on your insights and expertise to make their decisions.

Although being altruistic builds trust through activities that aren't directly related to your product or service, there are plenty of ways for businesses to add to their sharability by becoming a trusted resource. These are efforts that generally don't create immediate sales or revenue. Rather, they're tools your audience can use to share your expertise with their audience without the pressure of telling or asking someone to buy something.

Things like in-store events, blogs, article marketing, and media exposure all are powerful means for helping your audience share your message. (We'll go into more detail on the specifics in the tools section that follows.) Local farmers' markets are great examples of sharing in action! It doesn't matter if a vendor is selling beets or beeswax; that vendor is ready and waiting to talk to you, learn about your needs, and educate you. The vendors treat buyers and the merely curious with the same respect, knowing that in educating the curious they gain that person's trust in them and that person is more likely to try their product. Even when the end result is not a sale, that newly educated individual may share what was learned (and from whom!) with one or many in his or her own network. When you take the time to offer the non- or not-necessarily-revenue-generating services that surround your main revenue-generating product offering, you're putting your business in the best possible position to be shared with customers and noncustomers alike. You actually have the opportunity to recruit people who have never used (and might never use) what your company has to offer into your Brand Advocate Army—all because you took the time to share your knowledge and earn your audience's trust.

STAYING ON TOPIC ABOUT OFF-TOPIC CONVERSATIONS

When you're staying busy finding out what's important to your audience and asking how you can help them, you'll probably find yourself in conversations you never intended. Just think back to the last board or committee meeting (or meeting of any kind) you attended. Odds are, you weren't on topic the entire time. You talked about someone's trip to the emergency room with her son the night before, an inspiring video someone sent you, or a pressing political issue that's making news headlines in your community. Those things had nothing to do with the subject of your meeting, but everyone at that meeting went off topic in one conversation or another at one point or another.

That's because we're human and *those* are the things we find interesting. The off-topic conversation is how we relate to these other people in the room with us beyond the scope of coworker and into the realm of "This is someone I can work with." It's how we move someone from acquaintance to friend and from friend to lover. And it's also why women should probably skip walking into a first date in July sharing that they'd love to be married by Christmas. It's terrifying!

Nobody wants to do business with a one-track mind that's talking shop 24/7. As humans, we want to laugh and be entertained. We want to be able to see the brands we love and spend our money with people with whom we'd sit down and share a cocktail. Cocktails invite small talk, and that's how real people talk. When you give yourself permission to strategically go off topic, you humanize your brand in a way that few other strategies can.

And did I say strategically? There's little or no brand value in a children's hospital sharing a bawdy video on their Facebook page or in having the chief executive officer (CEO) of a software company go off on a rant in a public forum about the details of his or her divorce. So considering what's appropriately off topic is important. Think about what we discussed with brand personality: providing relief. Give your audience something that will take them away from the monotony that is their day-to-day lives. And although it's probably never going to be appropriate for a children's hospital to share a bawdy video, there may be an instance where it's appropriate for that software CEO to acknowledge an audience member who shares on Twitter that he is also going through a divorce or dealing with the loss of a pet or other personal challenge. It's relieving to find out that we're not alone in this wild spiral called life! When you can go off topic and lend value by providing relief, your audience will keep coming back time and time again—and not just when they need what you have for sale.

BUILDING THE LADDER TO THE ROOFTOPS—TOOLS FOR SHARING

So you're thinking of your audience first and imagining ways for your brand to be a trusted resource for customers and noncustomers alike. You know your audience well enough to put those things together and talk about topics that have nothing to do with your brand but everything to do with life. So how can we make it as easy as possible for our audience to get up on the rooftops from which we want them shouting? Well, we don't make them pull a Spider-Man and scale walls—we build them ladders! Ladders are the tools they they'll need to easily share their affection for your brand, and they span the digital, physical, and human realms.

- **Sharing Online:** Make sure that your website and blog have sharing options built in and let your audience share on their terms. These options can be everything from simple widgets that your developer can add to the back end of your website (like Digg Digg and AddThis, both social sharing plug-ins that let your audience share on nearly every social site imaginable) to letting people know how to find you across the web. If you have social profiles on sites like LinkedIn, Twitter, Facebook, Open-Table, Yelp, or the myriad of other sites out there, don't bury that information on the bottom of your web page or, heaven forbid, leave it off completely. Put it in a highly visible location and make it simple for your audience to both connect with you and then share you and the things you've created with the simple click of a button.
- **Sharing in Person:** It doesn't matter what kind of business you're running. Getting together with your audience in person is an invaluable opportunity. Create events that encourage your audience to share you. For retail locations, these can be occasions such as exclusive, invitation-only shopping events. Restaurants can establish loyalty programs and rewards through applications like Foursquare and Yelp, thereby giving audiences a reason to introduce a new friend to their location. (Giveaways such as a free cocktail on your first check-in work great!) Referral programs should also be a mainstay for service-oriented businesses such as hair salons and similar businesses. Let your

customers and clients know you appreciate their referrals and reward them for helping you build your business.

- **Recognizing Your Employees as an Audience:** The people who work with you side by side each day to get your business where it needs to go are often overlooked mouthpieces for your brand. Every one of your employees has his or her own audience, so make it worth their time to bring in referral traffic and empower them to share your brand! Although larger companies will likely feel the need to establish guidelines for how employees can act on the company's behalf (codes of conduct and social media policies), it's only to a brand's benefit to include its team in every sharing initiative possible. Just think of how many businesses or services you heard about from one of their employees. Now think of what that type of sharing could do for *your* brand.

TOOLS AND METRICS FOR SHARING

And as you go through the process of finding which tools work best to help your audience shout your message from the rooftops, you'll also want to understand *how* you're being shared so that you can refine future efforts and point your audience in the right direction. Here are some ways you can get a better handle on this:

- **Facebook:** How can you learn what your audience likes best about what you're doing on Facebook? Brand and Business Pages have built-in analytics called Insights designed to do just this. Although Facebook is constantly evolving its platform (and the Insights right along with it), there are a few resources you should always have on your radar to help you understand what's being shared, and how, by your Facebook fan base.
  - **Learning to Use Insights and Basic FAQs:** Do a web search for "using Facebook Insights" and you'll be taken to a web listing of all the resources available (even from Facebook itself) to get you up to speed on using and interpreting your fan/business page data.
  - **Shares:** In 2011, Facebook added a feature called Shares. For every post you make on your Page, you can now see how many times it's been shared by your audience. Although this might

change in the future (as everything with Facebook seems to), watching what's been shared the most gives you a better grasp on what your audience finds valuable, which can help you shape your future efforts to emulate your most popular content.

- ○ **Virality:** As of late 2011, virality was a new addition to the Facebook Insights platform. In Facebook's own words, this is the number of unique individuals who have created a story from your Page post as a percentage of the number of people who have seen it. The higher the percentage, the more popular the content—also useful for seeing the type of content your audience wants to share. You can also sort by photos, posts where you shared links, and more, which makes it easy to see how often people are sharing specific types of content on your page. You can also see how often people are sharing content that goes to your website versus other sites, which is great information if you have a business model dependent on converting website visitors into paying customers.
- **Twitter:** At the time this book was being written, Twitter had no publicly available analytics to help you understand who's sharing what or how often. That's where third-party applications come in handy. Platforms like awe.sm, HootSuite, CoTweet, and Argyle Social all have built-in analytics of varying degrees that can help you determine how often and to what extent your audience is sharing you. If you don't want to pay for one of these third-party services, you can use what's called a URL shortening service to provide you with data. Services such as Bit.ly let you take a URL from any website and shorten it into a link that not only helps you decrease the number of characters (since Twitter limits you to 140) but track the performance of that link. All you have to do is shorten the link using Bit.ly (or a similar service) and then log into your free account to track the link's performance. You'll see what's getting clicked on and how often, giving you more insight into what your audience has been compelled to share. The best way to find these services is to do a web search for "URL shorteners" and then review the latest products to see which one fits your needs.
- **Your Website and Blog:** Google Analytics remains the gold standard for understanding who's coming to your website, where

they're going once they arrive, and how long they stay. Specific to the conversation about sharability, there is a report available in Google Analytics under Content called Top Content. This report tells you what pages of your website or blog are receiving the lion's share of your audience's attention. It's also a good idea to take a look at a report in Analytics called Traffic Sources. Here, you can view everything from the websites that are referring the most traffic to your website and/or blog to how useful the social media outlets you've chosen to participate in are to bringing traffic to your site. When you combine the most popular content data with your traffic source data, you've got actionable information that helps you better serve your audience based on where they live and what they like. After all, *those* are the rooftops from which they're going to be shouting!

Visit the Resources section of the website for this book (www.unpopularbook.com/resources) and click on Chapter 5. There, you can view a brief video called "Google and Social— Tracking Down Your Traffic Sources" that demonstrates how to do this step by step.

- **Brick-and-Mortar Metrics:** When you run a business that relies on foot traffic, you need additional metrics to understand how people are hearing about you and how they arrived at your doorstep.
  - ○ **Employee Training:** Make sure that your staff is trained to ask how people heard about you and to let people know about any loyalty and referral programs you offer. They should also be trained to let your customers know where they can find you online, how to sign up for any mailing lists you offer, and otherwise stay in touch with your business when they're not *at* your business. Employees are powerful resources not only for sharing your brand message but also for relaying customer sentiment once they walk through the door. Your job is to empower them to help you compile the data you need to make better business decisions.
  - ○ **The Onus:** Never engage in any marketing effort that's not trackable in some way. The onus is entirely on you to know where your marketing dollars and efforts are going and what value they're bringing in exchange for dollars and time spent.

Social couponing programs all offer ways to track those dollars, whereas newspaper advertisements might be more difficult if you don't build in metrics into your ads for keeping track of redemption. Keep tracking in mind any time you explore a new marketing initiative and hold your vendors and service providers to timely delivery and access to that information.

A RECAP ON SHARABILITY

We've taken it. We created a brand story that the right audience will find irresistible.

We've broken it. We've been altruistic in our approach to our audience, developing a personality that can't think of anything more important than sharing.

We've shared it. We put out the welcome mat, invited people inside, and reinforced that they truly are a part of what we're building, and we both need and appreciate them. They've joined our Brand Advocate Army, becoming the voices of our brand.

They've loved it. Our Brand Advocate Army is living our brand story, digging our vibe, and shouting our message from the rooftops. We've even built them ladders so they can reach the rooftops with ease. And we've loved our brands enough to pay attention to what and how people are sharing, so we can emulate those practices and save valuable resources moving forward.

So, how do you feel so far about having built a brand that can both communicate with its audience and leverage their voice to share your message far and wide? The next step is deciding how to manage all of the new fans (users and customers) that our Brand Advocate Army delivers to our doorstep. But before we get into that . . . can I buy you a cold beer and raise a glass to an unpopular path well traveled thus far?

Let's head to New England and check in with an entrepreneur who, together with a team of investors and a revitalized Brand Advocate Army, has taken a regional brew from near-zero to hero in only a few short years. Talk about how understanding your audience, being altruistic, and going off topic can boost your reach with the people who love what you do. Definitely something worth raising a glass to. Let's drink it in.

CASE IN POINT: NARRAGANSETT BEER

"HI, NEIGHBOR!"—INSIDE THE SHARABILITY OF NARRAGANSETT BEER

From 1919 until 1967, Narragansett Beer owned a whopping 65 percent share of the New England beer market. Following an acquisition by Falstaff Brewing in 1965, however, the beer was headed toward becoming a forgettable brand as corporate possession took hold. But then in 2005, some new owners (including current CEO Mark Hellendrung) set their eyes on the former regional mainstay and acquired the 6,000-case-per-year brand. Their thoughts? This could be something. They just had to determine what it wanted to become.

Today, Narragansett is a 600,000-case-per-year brand, and they're not stopping there. They've just celebrated the brand's 120th anniversary, and Mark has some tips for brands looking to tap into what Narragansett's turned on: a brand shared without borders by the people who matter most—its customers.

Who Owns Your Brand?

The Narrangansett brand—it's not my brand or even our brand. It's a public trust. Our customers let us know what they want, and we listen to them every day. In order for us to take this brand from where it was when we acquired it to wherever it was that we hoped it could go, we realized we had to give the brand back to the people it had been taken from when Falstaff took over. This kick-ass, friendly brand had been ripped from the hands of the people who loved it most, and I'm not talking about the owners. It had

(continued)

(*continued*)

been taken from the community. So getting back into that community and letting them know that they were our number one priority, well, that's what we did.

There's No Silver Bullet

There are a lot of brands out there that are looking to launch or revitalize that have this delusion that there's going to be a silver bullet, that One Big Thing that will thrust their company into the limelight. And it's a challenge when you're running a company and people are asking what that Big Thing is going to be. But here's the thing: the big stuff comes and goes with a bang, and then what do you do when you can't hear the bang anymore? You're back to where you started. Whatever buzz you created dies off, and those people who came along with it will go by the wayside as well. The real return for us comes from things we do every day for the communities that surround our product.

In order for a brand to ever have the hope of being sharable, it has to make the commitment to engage with its community. And I'm talking immersion. Just opening your doors isn't enough. You have to be willing to live where they live and understand what's important to these people. Beer is inherently sharable. People drink it at events, with friends—but as a brand, we had to figure out what that meant to us.

Ultimately, it meant that we made the commitment to get involved in the communities where we distribute. I'm not talking bullshit bar promotions—I'm talking real community support of the culture that makes our customers who we are. We're based in Rhode Island, and Newport is a killer summer destination. The assholes from the big brands come in for two months during the summer, throw some promotions and bottle openers down with logos on them and then they're gone at the end of the season. The difference with us? We're doing that every day, 365 days a year, and we're doing it for our customers—not just to sell beer. People travel here from all over the country and the real payoff for us comes from being so involved in the community that when the guy visiting from Ohio leaves at the end of the summer, he changes his Facebook picture to one where he's holding a 'Gansett. Big-box brands don't get that kind of traction here, and the people they do get traction with from those crappy promotions aren't our customers anyways.

Success Stories

You're probably wondering what we did to get the guy from Ohio to love us so much that he couldn't wait to share. It boils down to one word: culture. In every town or city where we distribute, we make the conscious effort to dive into their culture. Our employees have been a huge part of this, too. We do a lot with local music and there are two people on our staff, Mat Medeiros and Zac Antczak, who have just taken their passion and involvement in the local music scene and made the Narragansett brand a part of it. If you want to know the scoop on the hottest new music venues or must-see musical acts, we've got that information and share it everywhere we can.

Marketing for us has always been about giving—and if we can help a musician by putting up some beer for his CD release party or getting the word out about some great shows, the community appreciates that. They know we share their stuff, and in return, we log into our social accounts every day and see new pictures uploaded from all of these events we support and people who love our beer.

(continued)

(*continued*)

Find What People Love

We've become such a sharable brand because we make sharing fun. A lot of that stems from figuring out what people love in every one of the communities where we distribute. There's a kickball team and cyclocross races in Rhode Island (and they race for beer), fishing tournaments, art gallery openings, and a whole bunch of stuff that crops up in between. We've shared our resources with these people who love doing all of these fun and amazing things and in return, everyone sees them drinking our beer, winning our beer, and our product finds a way into all of these pictures. It's great to see 'Gansett in the pictures, for sure, but the real payoff is when we continuously see our brand becoming an integral part of what our customers consider to be fun. We never want to stop receiving those requests for sponsorship, donations, and help with event promotions. Those are our customers telling us they want to share us. We'll never turn the volume down on that knob.

Knowing Your Culture

Truth be told, we're not after the customer who walks into the grocery store every Sunday right before game time and makes a price-motivated decision. Those big guys spend millions of dollars each year making sure people come to the cold beer case an hour before kickoff. Our target demographic is one that's open to experimentation and finds value in discovery. We'll never access that price-motivated audience, and we never really want to. Why would we want to compete on price when we have an entire culture of people who are interested in experimentation and the diversity of the beer industry? This is the audience we want, because they're completely into sharing what they've discovered. That's how new people learn about your brand and come to trust the information in the process. Are you going to buy something the first time because you saw an ad or because someone you trust said, "Hey—this is great. You should check it out." We thrive on sharing and because of it.

Tall Boy and Clammy

Maybe you think costume characters are cliché, but when it comes to sharing, they're huge for us. We have two characters: Tall Boy and Clammy. We send them out to various events, and there's no beer, no sampling. Just the characters. You get a real feel for how much people love your brand when they rush Tall Boy at every Red Sox game and wait in line to get pictures with him! Those pictures with high fives turn into posts on Facebook, tweets, and posts in other places. That's not brand love you can buy. You can only build it. And if people show us they love us by high-fiving and posing with two guys dressed up as a big can of beer and a clam, there's no way we're going to give that up in favor of some forced promotion where people can't share the love with their friends.

How Embracing Sharability Has Helped Them Grow Their Brand

In 2011, Narragansett expanded its brand into New York, Pennsylvania, and North Carolina. Mark shares that they owe much of their ability to do that through accepting that it wasn't *their* brand and that of all the voices out there, their audience's is the loudest. For example, they met with a bar manager down in North Carolina. This isn't a market where they advertised or

(*continued*)

(continued)

sent someone in to test the waters. They contacted Narragan-sett. The bar manager said that he'd heard the buzz about their beer and watched their progress online—through their social media efforts, press coverage, and bloggers in the beer community—and that he wanted his bar to be the launching point for Narragansett in the Raleigh-Durham market. Mark shares that part of him was thinking, "It's amazing that this guy even knows about us in the first place." The other part? "It's really thankful that we've given our audience the voice we have." They talk about their beer, get new people to notice them, and are a pretty hefty part of the reason they're in these three new markets this year.

Going back to knowing your culture for a minute—it's also been a key factor in the brand's ability to expand. For them to find success in a new market, they have to have distributors—and not just any distributor, but ones who will put the time and effort into helping them gain traction. The effort they put into making their brand accessible and sharable helps these key peo-ple so much. They can show potential customers how much Narragansett's investing from their side and how enthusiastic their customers are. When overall beer sales are flat in one particular area and one of these great distributors they've part-nered with can walk into a location and say it has Narragansett and everything that comes with the brand and that it's the only distributor who can get Narragansett into that particular establishment—that's powerful. Sharability doesn't just help you—it's something that benefits everyone you do business with.

Takeaway Tips for Any Business

- **Immerse yourself.** You can't hover above the surface of the community that you want to love your brand and what you offer. Get in there and get dirty. That's where you find the best opportunities to get involved, just as Narragansett did with their audience.

- **Make it easy to share.** If you're going to get on the social web, make sure people know where to find you. Facebook, Twitter, Yelp—whatever your poison—get people there and make them glad they came. Narrangansett does this by making sure every one of their fans knows where they live online and encouraging them to upload photos, one of the easiest pieces of media to share.

- **Talk back.** Their brand's costume characters high-five and their social web managers have conversations. It's a two-way street. Make sure you're running a two-way street with your target demographic, because the magic happens when interactions happen.

- **Forget the big bangs.** There's nothing wrong with running a bigger marketing thrust every now and then, but don't ignore the value of your everyday interactions with your audience. People share brands when they become a part of their lives, laughter, fun, and everything they look forward to. Your brand becomes a part of those things with the interactions you can engage in from a marketing perspective every day.

- **You have to share first.** Just like Narragansett got involved heavily in the music scene and events in their customers' communities, your brand has to take the first step. Who do you want to like you? What do they like? How can you become a part of it? Don't ask people to buy your product. Instead, start asking how you can help them enjoy the things that are important to them even more.

- **Think about relationships.** Everything your brand does affects everyone you do business with. When you make the entire package attractive for everyone who can help your

(continued)

(*continued*)
business find success—from your customers to the partners
you need for growth—you're doing better business than a
fair share of your competitors.

Narragansett Beer
Providence, Rhode Island

Website: www.gansett.com
Facebook: www.facebook.com/narragansettbeer
Twitter: @Gansettbeer

CHAPTER 6

SCALABILITY

*NEWS FLASH—YOU CAN'T DO
EVERYTHING YOURSELF*

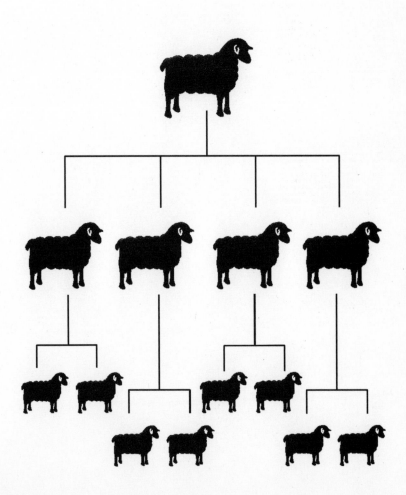

"Let's face it—growth can be frustrating and exhilarating. It's the most exciting thing you can see your company do when you have the infrastructure in place to support it. And it's terrifying when you see areas of the business crumble because someone wasn't paying attention to ensure the system could absorb the next stage of growth."
—Wendy Lea, CEO, Get Satisfaction

Following the unpopular path is designed to help you build businesses with a large dose of devil-may-care and help you find the people who can't resist your secret sauce. When you do it right, you're probably going to have a problem that many people would like to have: managing your business's growth. As entrepreneurs, we're naturally very driven people and assume more responsibility than the average bear. But I can speak from experience and say it's a rude awakening to realize that we can't do everything, especially when our businesses become more than we can handle alone. What might be an even more jarring thought is to acknowledge that we shouldn't even be trying to do everything. So riddle me this: How do you avoid blowing up your business when business explodes—and in a good way?

Investopedia defines *scalability* as a system's capability to cope and perform under an increased or expanding workload. For our purposes, scalability is about controlling your brand through growth stages and not letting it control you. The last thing any of us wants is to wake up one morning to realize that we've got this out-of-control, nine-headed hydra standing where the brand we love used to be. And the worst part? It's something we could have avoided if we hadn't spread ourselves too thin. We brands looking to harness the power of unpopular have to put the right infrastructure in place to handle all of the growth that comes our way; otherwise, we're not holding up our end of the bargain with our audience. If we built this business for them and can't continue to deliver our solutions because we crapped out on bandwidth, we've just done a whole lot of work—and disappointed a whole lot of people—for nothing. So let's talk about honoring our audiences through developing a sound infrastructure and then three major aspects that will affect if, when, and how we can scale: owning roles, building teams, and getting the business side of your business together.

FROM THE GROUND UP: IT'S ABOUT INFRASTRUCTURE

"We might be selling 50,000 cases of beer a year now, but we have to think about the mandated reality of how it all will work when we're selling 100,000 cases each year. You're building now to support what you know you'll later achieve."
—Mark Hellendrung, CEO, Narragansett Beer

Houses are framed. So are cars. Bicycles are pretty much 100 percent frame. Look around your house: there's nothing that's able to stand on its own that doesn't have a solid frame. Surprise! Your business is no different.

Ever wonder why there hasn't been a business book published about the Amoeba Concept or the Jellyfish Model? It's because they're not viable growth strategies. All of those ginormous unpopular brands in the world—the Zappos, Targets, Ellens, New York Yankees—they all have extremely defined infrastructures. The reason they're in place is so they can continue to do business, and business gets done only when we can deliver the product and service our customers have come to expect—and in the manner they've come to expect it. If we fail to do that, all of those ladders we built to the rooftops aren't going to do much good, because our audience is just going to go climb someone else's—someone who has the infrastructure in place to deliver.

Infrastructure is a means to accelerate growth. So if you're looking to grow your business, I'd be remiss not to make its development a priority. But you can't accelerate anything if you don't understand the role you play in your business. Most entrepreneurs (myself included) come to this realization in a true baptism-by-fire way, as we've been the ones who have driven concept to product and been everything from head cook to waitstaff. When growth is on the line, however, those aren't roles you need to be playing. It's time to acknowledge the role you *want* to play versus the ones you currently fill in your business.

OWNING ROLES

It's empowering to know that you're someone who takes on a metric ton of responsibility, but you can't identify where you belong in your company's infrastructure until you admit to yourself where you really want to be spending your time. As businesses develop, you invariably gravitate toward certain responsibilities and roles; granted, you find yourself picking up the slack in other areas, just because you don't have the resources to deal with those things. But in order to develop a resilient infrastructure, we need to own the role we want to play in the move-forward vision of our companies and find those other people who will handle the things we don't want to or are simply not good at doing.

You might remember Sy Sperling for his famous quote, "I'm not only the Hair Club President, but I'm also a client." He started Hair Club for Men in 1976 as a 20-something entrepreneur who was recently divorced and losing his hair. Twenty-four years later, he sold Hair Club to private investors for $42 million. The brand was then acquired again a short five years later by hair care industry giant Regis for $210 million. Given that Sy dedicated his life to building a brand that now services more than 50,000 people each year—with a straightforward, no-frills advertising methods that earned him a place in pop culture (how many entrepreneurs get to be guest on Leno and Conan O'Brien?)—I asked him what he felt was the biggest *mistake* he'd made while growing Hair Club. It had to do with owning his role and scaling his business and some decisions he made as a result. Here's what he said:

> When I started my company in New York City, I was in a small storefront salon. As I got bigger, I moved to a bigger salon. Then it was locations in other boroughs. Then . . . outside of New York State. I didn't have the expertise to become a national company, which is where I wanted my business to go. I think one of the smartest things you can do as an entrepreneur is realize your shortcomings.

He considered himself more of a sales and marketing guy and decided to own that role. And that's where Sy got himself into trouble.

BUILDING TEAMS

"I went out and I hired a Harvard MBA," he explains. "And let me be clear—I hired the *first* MBA that came my way. Everything looked great on paper and I needed the help, so away we went. As time went on, things weren't working out as I'd hoped and it was ultimately not a good fit—for me or my company. I should have gone through a better, more in-depth screening process."

We all have strengths, so when you've accepted the role you'll play in your growing brand, you have no choice but to build a team to get everything else done that needs doing. "I think of it like a baseball team," says Sy. "You need all of the positions in order to win the game. A field full of pitchers isn't going to do it."

Sy recovered from his staffing snafu and was still able to go on to build the perfectly unpopular brand—if you didn't understand the self-esteem issues associated with hair loss, you sure weren't going to understand Hair Club (and that was okay by them!). Hair Club's experiences demonstrate how much of a drag either a lack of resources or the wrong resources can be, so how can we take a page out of Sy's playbook and learn to build teams that will support our company's goals and create momentum?

- **Know your brand and hire people who believe in it.** The days are gone where you can afford to have someone who just "needs a job" representing your business. Every hire you make should be someone you trust to speak for (and well of) your company. You need people who are jazzed to come to work—not those who just show up.
- **Empower your team.** The collective job of your team members is to inspire one another, right along with building an unpopular brand that will inspire the right audience. You need to lay out the same welcome mat for your team that you did for your audience. This means enabling your team to offer unpopular viewpoints (and maybe disagree with the founders on occasion) with the goal of finding things that will move your business forward. No one you want to hire wants to work in a dictatorship, just as your audience doesn't want to be talked at. When everyone belongs, brands become very, very unpopular—because there are no limits to what your team can imagine and then accomplish.

- **Say thank you.** Smaller businesses might not have all of the whiz-bang benefits and perks of Fortune-rated giants, but you do have the power of "thank you." Although there might be some who would say that (especially in this economy) your team members should be thankful to just to have jobs, it's us as team builders and entrepreneurs who should be the thankful ones. We're people who are used to piloting our own ideas down a runway, so we need to continuously have the humility to thank the people who are committing their time to our goals. Saying thank you is inclusive—it brings your team to a more intimate level and establishes an undercurrent of respect. It's not a display of weakness; it's a show of respect. We need *everyone*.

Mentoring can also play an incredibly powerful role in your brand's development. Mark Hellendrung (whom we met in the last chapter's Case in Point) offers a great perspective that wraps up building your team.

> The most important investment a brand can make is in its people. I've been guilty on occasion of not putting as much into the front end of that as I should, but when you're a small company in the trenches every day, some things get missed. Huge companies have massive HR departments. You've got you. So when you think about scaling your business and the importance of building a team, think in terms of scaling yourself. If I can teach someone to do work in a more productive and efficient manner, I now have two of me.

And there's more than one way to build a team. All brands will have to make the decision of what to bring in house and what they'll keep outsourced. Regardless of their employee status, they're still a part of your team.

GETTING THE BUSINESS SIDE OF YOUR BUSINESS TOGETHER

Let's talk about overhead. Office space, employees, business equipment—what do you really need to spend your cash on in order to get ahead? Whether you decide to hire employees or use contract labor for certain positions is entirely up to you, but knowing what to outsource can help you keep overhead low. And lower overhead helps ensure you have the resources you need when growth comes calling (and demanding that you hit the *Spend* button). Outsourcing also gives you access to people whom you really have no need to hire full time, yet your business can't live without. It's time to get the business side of your business together. And it's important to remember that every one of us started at the beginning at one point or another. If you find you don't have a grip on some of the things that follow, now's a damn fine time to get grabbin'.

Your Business Entity

Are you walking around as a person, or are you presenting yourself as a business? If you want people to take you seriously as a business and brand, get a business entity ASAP. You'll want to consult with a tax professional to help determine which business entity is appropriate for not only the type of business you run but your particular cash flow situation as well. The most common types of business entities are limited liability companies (LLCs), S-corporations (S-corps), and corporations. If you need another reason to go out and get your business entity set up, speak with a business attorney about liability and how your business entity can help limit that liability. You know, so if shit hits the fan, people aren't coming after things like your house and other personal assets. Little things like that.

Your Business Licensing

You need to check and see what kind of business license your state, city, and county require. You can usually find this information on your state's Secretary of State website and at your city's Treasurer's office. Your business attorney and tax professional will also have this information and be able to help point you in the right direction. We are all parts of our local economies and should take the steps required to be not only active, but financially responsible participants.

Business Banking

Are you putting all of that money from your business into your personal bank account? Oh, heavens mercy me—no. Payment made to your company needs to be made payable to a business entity and go into a business banking account. And don't go using your business debit card or checkbook to go buy your kids shoes or pay your mortgage. Any tax professional will tell you that you need to keep your business and personal banking practices separate. The IRS doesn't like it when you don't, and failing to do so could result in the IRS saying your business entity isn't really a business.

Taxes

Your business's tax obligations need to be taken care of and kept in order. Most companies need to make quarterly tax payments based on that quarter's business receipts. It's a pretty big shocker at the end of the year to find out you owe a massive bill to the IRS and your state (if applicable), especially if you've recently left the world of being a W2 employee. Remember tax refunds? Those are pretty much a thing of the past once you become an entrepreneur. Keep your taxes straight and make sure you're setting aside money to deal with those obligations throughout the year.

Contracts

Seriously. If you're doing business without a solid set of contracts, you might as well be playing tennis naked—just waiting to get hit where no one *ever* wants to be hit. The amount of money you'll spend with a reputable business attorney to have a basic set of contracts drawn up will be money well spent, especially in light of what it could potentially cost you to do business without them. But hey—don't take my word for it. Head to Google and search for Mike Montiero's presentation called "Fuck You. Pay Me." It's less offensive than it might sound and takes a famous phrase from the movie *Goodfellas* and makes the case for why you should never (ever) work without a contract. If contracts don't apply to your business, it's still a hoot and definitely worth 39 minutes of your time.

If you're a start-up courting investors, it's even more important for you to have the business side of your business buttoned up right and proper. Although you'll have another world of documents and legalese waiting should you be among the fortunate who get investor dollars, the previous items are a solid start to be sure you're not doing business without covering your ass.

BUTTONING UP THE SCALABILITY CONVERSATION

While writing this book, a few colleagues thought that perhaps this chapter should have been placed before developing brand personality. Clearly, I said "nope," because if you don't build a brand that is personable, approachable, and sharable, growth isn't something you are going to have to be concerned with. So here it sits, fourth in the order of the five elements that are fundamental to a successful journey down the unpopular path.

As entrepreneurs, we're parents to our businesses. Parents give children infrastructure—everything from love to values to schools and life experience—that will hopefully help them make the best possible decisions as they grow. There might be the Terrible Twos and challenging teen years ahead, but we can get through those phases with at least some of our hair if we build our business to scale from the beginning.

Brands and their audiences need substantial care and feeding (which we'll get to in Chapter 9), but you won't be able to give your brand this kind of attention if you have to spend your time screwing around with things that should have been squared away from the get-go. Get your ducks in a row so that you keep hold of your brand as it finds a larger audience and demands for resources increase. It's exciting—watching something we've built take flight. The proper infrastructure lets us keep it in the air so that we can fly higher, longer, and more efficiently.

And speaking of ducks, let's talk to a guy named Craig Wolfe out of California. He knows a bit about scaling a business (multiple ones, at that)—and he's done it without hiring a single employee. Ever.

CASE IN POINT: CELEBRIDUCKS

CRAIG WOLFE ON ENTREPRENEURSHIP, HIS QUACK OF A BUSINESS CONCEPT, AND HOW NOT TO BLOW UP YOUR BUSINESS WHEN BUSINESS BLOWS UP

Craig Wolfe spied a framed, hand-drawn animation of Mickey Mouse hanging on the wall of a store one day in 1986 and was instantly captivated. "You could buy this stuff?" he thought. From that moment, he was consumed with figuring out where he could find this kind of art and how he could market it. These were pieces of Americana, created by Disney's greatest artists—and you could hang them on your wall. Surely, if *he* found these interesting, other people would as well. And he not only bet the farm on it, he built the farm, too.

Name That Toon went on to eventually become the largest publisher of animation artwork from television commercials in the United States and was responsible for all of those framed Coke, Budweiser, M&M/Mars, Kellogg's, Nabisco, and California Raisin artwork seen in homes and businesses around the country. For the 14 years Craig owned the business, it brought in annual revenues ranging from $250,000 to $1 million annually, but it wasn't all smooth sailing. Craig learned a thing or two about scaling a business right from the beginning—especially since he was the *only one* (no joke) looking to build a business out of selling animation artwork from all those famous television commercials.

Sometimes It's an Uphill Battle

Craig discovered early on that although his passion for creating a market for this animated art was well received by the companies who had created it in the first place, there was one small issue. "Once we were able to explain to these companies what

(continued)

(*continued*)

we wanted to help them do, they were completely gung ho on the concept of profiting from these wildly popular commercials. However, they didn't even know who had the original art files," he explains. Not only had no one ever come in before to tell a company, "Hey, I figured out a way for you to market these cool commercials you created!"—but no one had ever asked them for the art itself.

"In order for me to do the job I told these companies I could do, I needed that art. Not only did I need the art, but I needed the people who understood the technology required to take it from these new computer-generated methods to the printed page," says Wolfe. The key, he says, is coming to terms with knowing what you don't know and finding the people and resources to bring your vision to life.

It's Not What You Know; It's Who You Find

Craig's always built companies on lean operations coupled with a glaringly honest sense of humility. "I built a business that would—potentially—market commercial art to consumers, but I had no idea how to get that art from wherever it lived (which was, in many cases, computer files) to the place I needed it to be (acetate cels) to make it salable. With people asking for what I said I could deliver, I had no choice except to find the people who could help me scale—and fast."

Craig realized that these large companies outsourced the creation and production of their award-winning artwork to numerous studios throughout the entertainment industry, so it became his job to track down the studios, guns for hire that lived far out of the limelight. No one ever gave them credit for the animation they created or put their names front and center. That is, until Craig's company came along.

"I needed their brains—their know-how and technology to get the artwork they had into a medium I could use, so I was coming in with a pretty big ask," Craig explains. "I had to figure out what was in it for these animation and computer graphics studios. The way I saw it, the magic would be in taking them from behind the scenes and putting them in the spotlight. My plan was to put certificates on each piece of artwork we created, showing the edition number, and the name of the production studio that created this work on the front of the artwork itself! I offered them cobranding, which was something they'd never heard before. And it earned me a lot of new relationships that helped me build and continue to grow my business."

And it worked. Over the 14 years that Craig owned Name That Toon, he worked with some of the greatest names no one ever knew in the entertainment technology and art space, such as the people who brought the Coca-Cola polar bears to life, the masterminds behind the Gumby franchise, and the Academy Award–winning production talents of Stan Winston, one of the top model makers in the industry who brought icons like the Terminator and the dinosaurs in Jurassic Park to life.

What Was Next?

Craig had built Name That Toon into a licensed art empire, yet after all of the years spent on marketing other people's creations, he wanted to create something of his own. In 1998, he had an idea for a line of . . . wait for it . . . rubber ducks that looked like celebrities. His daughter, Rebecca, had recently graduated art school, and the two of them set about designing and manufacturing a prototype in Betty Boop's likeness. Leveraging his contacts from the manufacturing world, he had little Betty dropped off at the office of the head of licensing for King Features Syndicate, a company that handles the licensing for more than 150 comic strips, editorial cartoons, and games to more than 5,000 newspapers worldwide. A short while later, a call came in about Craig's "cute" duck. They wanted to talk.

CelebriDucks was born.

(*continued*)

(continued)

By the end of 2001, the company's annual revenue was in the $500,000 range, quickly escalating to millions of dollars in total revenues by the end of 2007. To date, the company has created ducks in the likenesses of some of the sporting world's most iconic players (Alan Iverson, Sammy Sosa, and Charles Barkley, to name a few), and more than a dozen Fortune 500 companies and national brands have commissioned custom ducks—Zappos, Kikkoman Soy Sauce, and Gorton's Seafood among them.

And here's the kicker: Craig Wolfe did all of this without ever having a single employee.

Become a Master at Outsourcing

"The quickest way to scale up without getting your ass kicked is through outsourcing," says Craig. His best advice to any brand in the making is to understand what you don't know and work from there to find the people to fill in the gaps. It doesn't matter what you're looking for—a bookkeeper or an entertainment industry computer-generated imagery (CGI) guy who can take computer animation and transfer them to acetate—those people are out there. You need to know enough about what they do and how they do it to so that you can determine whether you're getting their talent at a fair price and price your products and services accordingly. There's also a huge amount of trust that comes along with outsourcing, knowing that you're relinquishing some level of control to get something you need in return.

So how do you find this talent? Use the world as your human resources department. As Craig explains, "Your best people aren't necessarily going to be in your neck of the woods. If you have to fly them all out to one location and put them up in a building, you'll significantly increase your overhead. Do you really need that overhead? While that's the right decision for some brands at some point, I'm a big advocate of virtual work-forces. Ninety percent of the people who have worked and still work for my companies could walk by me on the street and we would not necessarily recognize one another. However, if we struck up a conversation, I'd know them in a heartbeat from the sound of their voices!"

An Interesting Side Effect to Outsourcing

Craig's always had a knack for knowing what to outsource, which has been nearly everything. As a lifelong believer in doing good business, his outsourcing has had an interesting side effect: his scaling concerns from a human resources standpoint pretty much take care of themselves. "I'm never at a loss for talent," says Craig. "When you're growing your business, you inevitably start working with more and more people. And when you do good business with those people, they're going to tell their colleagues. I have incredible talent lined up to help me whenever I need it. It's a pretty great thing to go to work every day and know that your customer's demand is never going to be compromised by your ability to supply."

If you have to micromanage everything, you're not going to have the time to deal with everything you need to deal with—bottom line. "When you get the best people—ones you can trust—regardless of location, you've just given yourself permission to build a brand based on a great business model. Believing in your customers starts with believing in the people you have powering your business. Trust starts inside and works its way out."

On Overhead

Since we live in a world where technology headlines are pushing the latest *this* and *that* every day and appearances in business can be overvalued, Craig recommends taking a hard look at where your business is spending its cash. You might want the latest technology, but does your business really need it in order to operate in a significantly more efficient manner? The word

(continued)

(*continued*)

significantly is crucial here. When you can keep your expenditures at a minimum while producing the best possible product, you keep control of your brand through those harried growth phases. "Let your business push you to the next step. It's doubtful that a new, expensive laptop is going to do enough pushing to make it worthwhile in the beginning," Craig offers.

The CelebriDucks website is not overly complex, especially by current web publishing standards, but Craig knows that and it's upgrade is on the "eventually" slate. "Do we need a new one now? No. It's a place that gives people a way to contact us, get a sense of who we are and what we're about, and maybe even buy some ducks. But at the end of the day, our core business gets done on the phone, so the phone number is the single most important thing there, aside from the ducks of course."

When it comes to the question of office space, some brands find real estate to be an understood necessity, but there are many businesses that can keep this expense at a bare minimum as well. Craig certainly doesn't think it should be one of a brand's first decisions. "If your business can outsource people *and* real estate, you'll find yourself way ahead of the game." And if you're building a business that eventually finds itself in need of both employees instead of contractors and office space instead of a home office, that's fantastic. Just make sure that you understand the implications on your overall business model, because you're probably going to see some pricing and procedural adjustments becoming a priority.

Put Everything into Your Brand

"I think it's curious that people want to promote themselves before they've done anything," Craig muses. "If you think about many of the incredible brands that change our lives and the people behind them—Apple and Steve Jobs, Microsoft and Bill Gates, Virgin and Richard Branson—the brands do and always have come first." You can't grow a company if your ego is in the way. Everything Craig's mentioned so far requires humility. "If you're a personal brand, people will pick up on that. You don't have to shove it down their throats." Forcing anything as your business is growing is a losing scenario. When the brand comes first, the brand will be there when you come out the other side of your growth phases.

"How easy would it be for me to be another Me Too product?" Craig asks. "Plenty. Do you know how many companies are out there making rubber ducks?! I had a very conscious decision to make as CelebriDucks started to take off: Was I going to fight it out at the low-price end with all of the other duck people, or was I going to keep my product vision on track and create something totally different that people would actually hold on to? Was I going to continue to produce something that people loved and kept talking about or something that often got discarded in short order or turned into a dog toy when people got it home? It was an easy decision to make. When you take the easy way out in the name of costs and ego, you let your brand run you. As an entrepreneur, you should always be the one running your brand."

Takeaway Tips for Any Business

- **Trust.** If you own your business for any period of time, you're likely to come across the occasional bad egg, especially while in growth phases. Forgive yourself for missteps and keep an eye on the brand and its goals. Focus on doing good business and finding talented people you can trust. You need people who share your work ethic and vision to move forward.

- **Become a better communicator.** Scaling your business requires exceptional communications skills. Some people are naturally great communicators, and other people have to work at it a bit more. Pick up the phone, get on Skype,

(continued)

(*continued*)

or go see someone in person. Figure out what works best for the people on your team and avoid a communication breakdown. Those breakdowns are some of the most avoidable instances we face in business. They're also detrimental to a shared vision, something required for any brand to survive growth.

- **Stay involved.** One of Craig's largest customers called one day and asked, "If you're the largest publisher for this type of artwork in the country, how come I get *you* on the phone every time I call?" Although Craig's strategically scaled his business using contractors, he's never forgotten the importance of being there and being involved day in, day out. "If I don't talk to my customers and get to know them, who will?" Scaling isn't about disconnecting. It's about giving your company the resources so that each person on your team can connect in a deeper, more meaningful way that's in line with his or her specific role.

CelebriDucks
San Rafael, California
Website: www.CelebriDucks.com

CHAPTER 7

PROFITABILITY

THE MONEY'S GOTTA COME FROM SOMEWHERE

Everything eventually comes down to money, doesn't it? The personality, approachability, sharability, and scalability—we've invested in all of these strategies so that we place ourselves in the best possible position to build businesses that will eventually put money where it needs to go: our bank accounts. So we should probably talk about what's *not* going to happen when it comes to money once you've set out to build the unpopular brand.

No flying monkeys will magically appear carrying large bags of $50s.

Leprechauns will not sneak into your house at night and modify your business plan so that you're instantly profitable (in fact, leprechauns suck at business plans).

There will be no man in a white hat who comes riding along on his trusty steed, keeping watch on both the prairie and you to make sure you're running a business and not a free clinic.

If you were running a free clinic, you wouldn't be expecting to get paid by anyone. But you *do* expect that. You provide a service. You have *value*—value that you need to figure out how to turn into bill-paying revenue. So, let's make sure that you're building a business that has the potential to bring in money instead of inadvertently turning yourself into a not-for-profit organization in the truest and most tragic sense of the phrase.

We'll break this down into the following guiding principles: *

- **Your time:** What it's worth, who gets it, and ways to think about spending it.
- **Getting things done:** It's cash or trade, and only one of them can pay your bills.
- **Pricing, discounts, and the risk of commoditization:** Why most entrepreneurs start out making pricing mistakes and how to quit that shit—and fast.
- **Emotional profitability:** Yes, this is an actual issue.
- **Embracing your value:** Taking everything above and using it to guide future time and financial decisions so that you can skip the rubber gloves and put on the boxing gloves instead.

As entrepreneurs and the driving forces behind brands, we have to be smart about how we spend our time, arrange finances, and

149

get business done so that we can keep doing what we love. We built an infrastructure in the last chapter to honor our audiences and their expectations. It's time to honor our passions by figuring out how to translate them to a bottom line that's (eventually) in the black.

YOUR TIME

Chapter 1 cited a quote from Thoreau that addressed wealth as being measured by the number of things we can afford to leave alone. As leaders of unpopular brands, we understand that the process we've just undergone (and scaling in particular) is designed to do just that—allow us to leave certain things alone. As your audience demands the majority of your attention, time comes at a premium. How should you spend it?

First of all, people will always want to "pick your brain" and find other ways of getting your hard-earned pearls of wisdom for less than they're worth. If you charge $5.28 per hour, then it's perfectly within reason for you to give someone advice for the cost of a cup of (pricey, fair-trade, roasted with the horn of a unicorn) coffee. Having spent entirely too long indulging in this practice with my own business, I can offer some pointers for triaging the things that are worth your time so that you can spend your time where it's needed most: directing your company toward its revenue generation goals and all of the aspects of personality, approachability, sharability, and scalability that will get you there.

- **Limit your investment prior to payment.** Regardless of the type of business you run, you need to clearly define what you're willing to give away for free. Are you really going to spend the time crafting a 30-page proposal only to find the client is going to shop you based on price? Although every business is a service industry in some sense, we don't have to feel obligated to bleed our time and resources just to gain someone's business. Something I found in my own business was that oftentimes the price I ultimately charged a client for a product or service didn't even begin to cover the time I'd invested in *acquiring* their business. So I'd ended up working for free.

- **Set rules for yourself.** My time is worth more than that $5.28 cup of coffee, so yeah—I generally skip coffees, lunches, drinks, and other ploys to buy my time and thoughts for less than they're worth. I've found that a 15- to 20-minute introductory phone call helps me clarify whether someone's needs are a fit for my expertise and whether I'm interested enough in their business to learn more. These might not be your exact rules; you'll have to establish your own guidelines. But you don't walk into a restaurant and ask to try an appetizer sampler for free to help you decide whether you want to have dinner there. Whatever your type of business, there are guidelines you can set for yourself that both address a client's or prospective client's needs and protect the use of your time. And you can have drinks and coffee! But I'm betting you can find a way to do business and grab a beverage without wasting your time.
- **Have the tough conversations.** Your time is precious, and you have to spend it on things outside of your business as well— friends, family, the community, and (oooh, yeah!) yourself. If you find that someone isn't being respectful of your time, have the tough conversation. The alternative is to continue letting that person, client, or customer continue wasting your time. And that sucks. It's your business—*you* set the rules.

You can't build a profitable company if you spend more time on things that aren't profitable than you do on things that are. Sure, there will always be things we'll need to do in order to earn and retain our audience that don't have immediate financial benefit, but owning your time and how you spend it keeps you out of the free clinic business and in the business you want to be in.

GETTING THINGS DONE

There are two ways to get things done in business, aside from doing them yourself: pay someone to do them for you or have them done in trade. Given that not a single one of my utility companies nor the IRS accepts trade as payment (the bastards), trading services is straight-up B.S. and something you should avoid at all costs. Yes, there are many people out there who have had success with trade situations. But as a general rule, unless you approach a trade situation like any other business transaction—bound by a contract or other terms of engagement–there will inevitably be one party that feels they did more than the other and didn't get a fair shake. And since you can't pay your bills, employees, contractor, or even parking meters with trade, cash really is king.

The beauty of cash is that it levels the playing field and you can use it to pay for . . . well . . . everything. You just have to make sure enough of it is coming in the door. That's a factor of your pricing model.

PRICING, DISCOUNTS, AND THE RISK OF COMMODITIZATION

The prices you establish for your business's products and/or services have to include more than just the cost of the item and the time you spend completing the actual task. I'm talking about overhead—that's Economics 101. It's everything from your business taxes and licensing to the cost of the time involved in acquiring the business. You have to account for any wages to outsourced subcontractors or paid employees and make sure that the piece that's left for you makes it worth your while to be stuck in the middle. If you're charging a fair value for your services, you should never feel guilty about your price tag.

So, Erika, Tell Us How You Really Feel about Pricing

Building an unpopular brand is a process designed to vet. You weed out the people who will never love you, get rid of business ideas that don't work, and develop a clear understanding of both your brand and audience that keeps you from bringing on team members who will be more a hindrance than a help. After you've gone through all of that work, why the hell would you put yourself in a position where you can't make money? Here's the skinny on how I feel about pricing:

- Not everyone will be able to afford you.
- Not every request will fit into your schedule.

- Clients are paying for your expertise, time, product, and energy—together, they create your product.
- If you give away your expertise for free, you devalue your brand and yourself.

It's your responsibility as savvy entrepreneurs to research your industry and establish pricing policies that offer the appropriate balance between market rates and expertise. So now is a pretty good time to discuss discounts, as the world will never be at a loss for people who price shop or otherwise want to get something for less.

Discounting and the Risk of Commoditization

We all have favorite stores that we'll go to regardless of price. We love the brands and how we feel when we get exactly what we came for—those are value-motivated decisions and the pricing is secondary. If there happens to be a sale when we arrive, it's a bonus. It's not the primary motivation for our patronage.

On the other hand, we also have those stores at which we never make a full-price purchase. Why? As consumers we've been conditioned to wait for the X-percent-off coupon that arrives in the mailbox like clockwork. As a consumer, you walk through stores like these and immediately do the 20-percent-off math on every product you pick up and wouldn't be caught dead in there without a coupon.

If you choose to offer a discount strategy, your clients can perceive it one of two ways: as a reward or as an expectation. It all comes down to how you set expectations. Do those giant stores offering the never-ending supply of X-percent-off coupons make money? You bet. But until you can run a volume-based business with hundreds of locations, you might want to skip the ever-present discounting strategy. But what about the periodic discounts—such as ones available through social couponing programs like LivingSocial or Groupon?

On Social Couponing—Is It Worth It? These deals are a great way for businesses to (potentially) reach a wider audience and can be hugely influential in driving new foot traffic to brick-and-mortar locations. But if you as a business participate in these, how do you know if you're getting a great deal or a raw one?

A report issued by the Social Science Research Network in June 2011[1] revealed the following statistics about 324 businesses in 23 markets that had participated in daily deals:

- A total of 55 percent of businesses reported making money, 26.6 percent lost money, and 17.9 percent broke even.
- A full 80 percent of deal users were new customers, although a rough 20 percent spent more than the actual deal value.
- A total of 48.1 percent of businesses indicated they would run another daily deal promotion, 19.8 percent said they would not, and 32.1 percent said they were uncertain.

Given that daily deal sites take on average 50 percent of the deal value and generally offer deals at up to 50 percent off of retail, brands can be left with as little as 25 percent of fair-market value for their product or service. If you're going to consider using a daily deal promotion, make sure not only that you have the pricing structure in place to withstand the cost compromise but that the one in five chance of obtaining a repeat customer is worth the expense. It's also wise to reach out to similar businesses in your area that have done social couponing and get their feedback.

When you discount and try to compete on price, you run the risk of commoditizing yourself and your brand. If you're building a business designed to compete on price, that's great—it's a part of your brand goals. But most of us aren't. Outside of couponing programs, what do you do when you're asked to offer the same product or service for less than your going rate?

The decision is ultimately yours, but discounting from the start is a bad practice in my eyes.

---

[1] Dholakia, Utpal M., "How Businesses Fare with Daily Deals: A Multi-Site Analysis of Groupon, Livingsocial, Opentable, Travelzoo, and BuyWithMe Promotions" (June 13, 2011). Available at SSRN: http://ssrn.com/abstract=1863466.

In a conversation with Stephen Denny, author of *Killing Giants: 10 Strategies to Topple the Goliath in Your Industry,* Denny offered up a simple piece of advice: **tell me what you're willing to walk away from.** Definitely something we can all do ourselves the favor of asking more often—and not just when it comes to being paid for what we do.

And you certainly don't have to accept work that's below your normal rate because the economy sucks. What about *your* economy as a business owner? If a client wants to haggle over price, there are two options to pursue:

- If you truly want to work on the project, offer a project discount. Offering 10 percent off your regular rates is more than fair, and 15 percent if you're working with a nonprofit organization.
- Explain that these are your rates. I'm fortunate that I rarely have to defend my pricing, yet when I do, I say one thing and one thing only: "I'm not the least expensive professional you will find, but you can get work that's significantly crappier for a lot more money." Get reviews, testimonials, and endorsements from your current and existing clients, and let your audience speak to the fact that you're worth every penny.

The "state of the economy" is no reason to discount what you do for a living. You can't haggle with the gas company or tell the supermarket you'd like to pay less for Cheerios because the economy is in a less-than-optimal state.

As you go through your pricing strategy and determine your worth, step back and take a good hard look at your table and everything you bring to it that justifies the price you charge. Building an unpopular brand is about demonstrating the value you bring to both your audience and the marketplace. Although great value can be influenced by price, price is rarely the sole indicator of value.

WHAT DETERMINES VALUE?

It's hard to build a profitable business if we aren't clearly able to communicate the value our solution offers our audience. That's why the chapter on profitability sits in fifth position among the five qualities that contribute to highly unpopular yet successful brands.

When you invest in the unpopular path, you're investing in your brand's value. You know the value that you bring to market, and it's up to you to make sure that you price your goods and services such that you have the fuel to keep on keepin' on the path both you and your audience love. Value drives profit, and profit's the fuel that keeps a business going. It lets us hire the team we need so that we can afford to leave certain things alone and, consequently, profit in ways other than those we deposit in the bank from the brands we build.

THE OTHER TYPE OF PROFITABILITY

Unpopular brands are fueled by our ridiculous and inconvenient love for new ideas and the satisfaction we receive from having both the opportunity and the latitude to give them a go. They're a substantial emotional commitment as well. They keep us up for long hours, can make those things other people refer to as "weekends" sound like a foreign language, and drive us to sacrifice a part of ourselves to the process of getting things done and driving our vision forward.

But what if it all blew up tomorrow?

Although you get the rush from creating, iterating, and living your dreams, how worthwhile do all of your efforts turn out to be if you sacrifice your relationships with the people—friends, family, spouses, children—who make the hours you spend away from your business emotionally rewarding? When you're involved in something that offers you no emotional opportunity for profit, what place does it deserve on your priority list?

Having put everything I had into a business—emotionally, physically, intellectually, and financially—only to see it fail (and for multiple reasons), I know what it feels like to give everything yet forget about our most important audience—ourselves. I left that venture out of shape and exhausted, with no social life, a failed relationship in its wake, and with more regrets than I had *atta girls*. And I don't care if you're a guy and you think this stuff about people and relationships is just huggy-speak. You're not above it. Although your business ventures might feed your entrepreneurial natures, people—your audience, loved ones, friends—feed your emotional energies. Don't ignore them. It's a rude awakening when you suddenly find you've ignored them for too long and they've moved on.

That's a pretty good segue into the start-up community and its specific needs regarding profitability. Although we're all starting a business at one point, start-ups have some special circumstances that dictate how, and how quickly, they're built to become profitable.

STARTING UP—A DIFFERENT FINANCIAL LIFE CYCLE

Different types of businesses will have specific nuances with regard to how they approach profitability. The start-up community has its own set of nuances—ones that demand that I speak to their particular needs individually. Although there's much that every type of business can borrow from others that will benefit their respective brands, a tech start-up (and start-ups in general) should be less concerned *initially* with making money than validating their business model's opportunity to eventually create an appreciable revenue stream. At the end of this chapter, we'll meet Josh Felser. As a serial entrepreneur and cofounder of Freestyle Capital (a San Francisco–area seed-stage investment firm), he has solid advice for any type of business on charting a path for eventual profitability. For start-ups, however, there are some specific pearls of wisdom you can take to the bank.

I listen to a ton of start-up pitches each year, whether directly from clients or at one of several conferences I attend. Anyone who does this with any regularity develops a knack for picking the companies and founders who *get* the power of unpopular. The five previous chapters and overall principles surrounding the unpopular brand are tools needed by every start-up and can help you position your company above the noise. Yet profitability—it's a delayed goal for you, as it should be.

"When companies are forming to solve a problem, whether it's one the marketplace is already addressing or not, they need to think about the team they're building. We always ask, 'Why this team?' because we consider the team to be more important than the business concept itself.

*Teams can persist while business ideas fail, and we want to know a
company we're investing in has the best possible team to put this solution into the marketplace."*

—Jason Mendelson, managing director and cofounder,

The Foundry Group

Every angel investor and venture capital firm is different with regard to funding preferences, but they're all looking for one thing in a
prospective portfolio holding: the potential for a company to make
them money. If their investment in you can't conceivably be returned
for (substantially) more than they put in, you're not a good risk. It's a
matter of math. Although they might be able to mentor and make
you better entrepreneurs, they can't take a business concept without
an appreciable potential for revenue and assume its risk as a portfolio
holding.

Getting the funding you need might require some shifts to both
your business model and audience base. Josh will go into this in
more detail, but here are his words of wisdom for start-ups who find
their revenue potential limited—as it's usually a factor of the size of
your audience: "When you build a small audience and you see it's
not working, the worst mistake you can make is to try to iterate on
that small audience. Scrap the idea, go back to the drawing board,
and do it while you have the cash to rebuild." It doesn't mean you
didn't come up with a great idea—it just means that the audience
attracted to your solution isn't large enough to (eventually) be attractive to investors and potential acquirers. Murder your darlings
and head back to the drawing board. No matter what kind of
business you run, your audience will always dictate the potential for
revenue and eventual profitability. As a start-up founder, you just
have other people to consider in the profitability equation, as you're
asking for other people's money to see your vision through.

STRAIGHT FROM THE WALLET'S MOUTH

We've gone through the value of your time, looked at cash versus
trade, and discussed pricing considerations relevant to any business. I
even made you get huggy, demonstrating that there's such a thing as
emotional profitability and that all of the other shit we do doesn't

matter if you don't have people in your life to share it with. So to back it all up, let's get you introduced to a professional "wallet." We're going to take emotional profitability and put it together with that whole audience thing—because that's truly what creates the potential for profitability. This guy should know—he doesn't just invest in companies. He and his partner invest only in companies with this key combination—as those are the ones they believe have the true potential to become profitable.

CASE IN POINT: FREESTYLE CAPITAL

TWO SEED-STAGE INVESTORS, AN ENTREPRENEUR, AND SOME CASH WALK INTO A BAR . . .

How Confidence and Audience Create the Potential for Profit

Josh Felser and Dave Samuel are serial successful entrepreneurs. Back in 1997, they founded Spinner, the first multichannel Internet music service, and in 2004, they founded Grouper, one of the first Internet video networks.

Those two efforts paid off to the tune of $320 million and $65 million, respectively, when they were each acquired less than three years following inception. As two guys who love nothing more than being entrepreneurs, they were challenged to find the ideal balance between the always-on mentality that fuels founding start-ups and needing to actually have the time to enjoy life. They were ready to found their next company, but how could they found one that had the balanced culture they wanted?

They opted for what they saw as the next best thing to a start-up: investing in entrepreneurs who were building companies they could support. Freestyle Capital opened its wallets

(continued)

(*continued*)
(read: Josh and Dave opened *their* wallets) in 2009. After two years of funding out of their own pockets in order to make sure (1) that it was something they continued to be passionate about doing and (2) that it was working and something they were good at, they decided to raise capital. In May 2011, they closed their first fund. Freestyle now holds 28 companies in their portfolio, and of those 28, 6 have been acquired. These are two guys who know not only about successful entrepreneurship but how to mentor other entrepreneurs toward a path of real revenue potential. Josh shared his insights with me on profitable companies, from both a financial and emotional standpoint.

A Word on Confidence

"It's inevitable that entrepreneurs who start a business extrapolate from their own experiences," says Josh. "Some of those experiences don't translate into a sense of confidence and security. Recognizing that, something that we do that's different from many of the other VCs [venture capitalists] out there is act as a sort of life coach to the entrepreneurs in our portfolio companies. When an entrepreneur is comfortable in his own skin, it reflects across every decision he makes for his company. We do what we can to help the founders of our portfolio companies gain that confidence, while keeping the humility they're going to need to let the business grow the way it's supposed to."

A Different Perspective on Profitability

Because Freestyle invests primarily in companies with strictly virtual footprints, they offer an inside perspective for the start-up community. "It's different for the hyperlocal, local, and regional business owners than it is sometimes for a start-up when it comes to profitability," says Josh. "When you're brick-and-mortar or local in some way, you have a defined audience that's going to contribute to your bottom line. On the start-up side, you're probably looking at a broader audience scope since so many of those companies offer virtual products and services. But no matter what side you're on, the potential for profitability comes from focusing your business model on a big, saleable audience. Simply being big doesn't usually cut it, anymore."

Will you "make money" right from the get-go? Probably not. That's not the primary goal for most start-ups, as they're still in the process of developing their products and services. That development phase, however, doesn't preclude the need for you to answer the needs of a wide enough audience to make it viable. It all starts with your audience. "If you find yourself in a situation where your audience is getting in the way of the potential for revenue—such as they're as big as you initially thought and, therefore, not big enough to create a future potential for appreciable revenue—you need to be comfortable enough in your own skin to burn it to the ground," Josh states. "You have to go back and rebuild your audience to have the chance for your concept to succeed." And this speaks to the cyclical nature of the unpopular brand's development cycle. Audience is key, so its continual reassessment will tell you if they're a factor in your ability to become a profitable company.

So what does Josh recommend entrepreneurs be aware of in taking care of the profitability potential of their respective businesses? We'll break it down into two different areas: emotional and practical.

Emotional Profitability

- **Explosive Passion:** It's a must for every entrepreneur, no matter what kind of business you're running. If you're not passionate, you can't be inspirational—and part of your job as a founder is to inspire your audience every day. And remember that your audience includes everyone from your team to investors to your target demographic. And you

(continued)

(*continued*)

can't fake this. You have to be authentic about what excites you and what makes you nervous, and when you lose passion, you lose the desire to collaborate and share. That kills your product, which ultimately can kill your company. Profitability—right out the window.

- **Humility:** Sometimes entrepreneurs face the difficult reality that their brands need to grow in a direction that's best for future revenue potential and audience satisfaction, but it not be one they initially envisioned as founders. So the second you find you're not passionate about the direction your own company has to take, find your replacement. Get ahead of that decision-making process, because you always want to be the instigator in that action. Companies have to grow in order to have the chance at profitability, and it's okay for those directions to not always be the best ones for you personally. No argument—it's a tough place to be in, and you won't know what it feels like until it happens to you. But think about the audience and team you've built and whether, should passion fade, you're the right person to keep the company on course.

- **The Catalyst:** Think about your company in terms of investors. Some local businesses might see their patrons as their investors. Start-ups are more often than not looking for funding of some sort to bring their business to that next level. Every investor needs a reason to invest—a catalyst. Your responsibility as an entrepreneur is to create a catalyst that makes an investor focus on your business, and *now*. Why now? Because *meh* is dangerous. There are so many businesspeople out there looking to get the attention of the same investors that you have to be the business that explains your *why us* with both clarity and a sense of urgency. Rise above the noise. The entrepreneurs who can create the catalyst see more foot traffic, patrons, or users. They see more investors. Period.

Practical Profitability

- **Managing Cash Flow:** Having a good handle on when you're going to run out of cash is imperative. Although it might seem like a no-brainer, it's truly astounding how many companies find themselves surprised by their cash position. Know your burn rate and what you're burning it on and how much time you have left before you're going to need more money. No one's going to keep track of that for you.

- **Raising Capital:** If you're a company that needs to fund-raise, plan ahead. Know when your cash is going to run out and plan to start fund-raising six months in advance of that date to avoid putting your company at risk. In the start-up space, more product progress can lead to higher valuations, so some companies can really walk the line between showing progress and running out of money. We've found that the best time for start-ups to head out and start raising that next round of funding is six months from the date they anticipate they'll run out of money. This timeline offers potential investors maximum value and companies minimal risk.

  And keep in mind that your product timeline and funding timeline should be in sync. If you're heading out to seek funding at your company's six-month-from-ground-zero point, you should have some recent product or company developments scheduled to come to fruition at that time. Show progress. Investors find progress—new product releases, press coverage, partnership announcements—potentially catalyzing and your ability to raise funds will most likely be directly related to how you can convey that progress.

  If you're not a start-up and are looking for investors or funding through things like Small Business Association (SBA) loans, the six-month window is still a safe bet. It ensures you can get through application and due diligence processes and still have the cash you need to keep your business intact if things run longer than you planned.

(*continued*)

(*continued*)

The Biggest Mistakes?

Josh has one leading mistake that he sees in the marketplace when it comes to profitability—and for some, it might seem counterintuitive. "It's so inexpensive to build a company in today's economy that we see companies making a huge mistake of not spending their cash fast enough. When you're too frugal and you aren't spending and hiring the people you need in order for your company to make progress, you've got no shot at profitability. You're going to run out of money before you have the chance to build something that your audience will love, share, and buy."

He's definitely not advocating that entrepreneurs burn through their cash for the sake of burning it or with a sense of panic and needlessly increasing overhead. It's more a matter of scalability: every entrepreneur requires a team to get his or her company from point A to point Z. Spend wisely and when cash is available, investing in the resources that have the best possible potential to move your business forward. Forward is the path to profitability, and there are no jet planes or bullet trains that can get you there faster.

Freestyle Capital
Mill Valley & San Francisco, California
Website: www.freestyle.vc
Twitter: @joshmedia and @dsamuel

CHAPTER 8

FINALLY—THEY HATE ME!

Remember when we talked about the given that you're guaranteed to piss people off when you decide to create an unpopular brand? Yep—still true. But given that you've read this far, you might still be interested in how we can leverage both the people who will never love us *and* the people who we may have riled up but who still do love us to continue to build smarter brands.

As I was doing the research for this chapter (and this book in general), I met so many incredible entrepreneurs who reinforced the power that's inherent in the entrepreneurial community and the reasons why we should all be focused on unpopular business tactics. They responded to my queries about brands that found ways to leverage negative sentiment into positive outcome; and even though I was expecting them, I still was surprised with the overwhelming number of responses I received. Entrepreneur culture is one deeply seated in sharing—both the good and bad about the business world. They don't live in a land of wishes and unicorns, and they know that especially when it comes to serving their brand's reason for being—their audience—every brand's going to have to find a way to take its lumps.

Whether we can create something palatable out of those lumps is completely up to us.

This chapter takes a path that none of the others have—the case studies *are* the chapter. I had an entirely different draft originally—neatly sorted with gorgeous subheadings and poignant prose explaining how we should approach the inevitable negativity surrounding any unpopular brand. And then I killed it. There was nothing I could say that was more powerful than the insights that came directly from these entrepreneurs who are just like you, so I've simply arranged them with light introductions and conclusions and let the material speak for itself. Let's begin with Mike Masin, owner of @Stuff LLC (www.atstuff.com), a technology firm that makes e-commerce easier, smarter, and more profitable for companies needing those services. He sums up the types of negative feedback any entrepreneur might encounter, along with what you can do about each sort.

There are three types of customer feedback; one of them can save your business:

"We love you; keep doing what you're doing!"
That's always great to hear and it feels good, but it doesn't help you grow because you already know what you're doing right.

"We hate you, we won't talk to you again, and don't bother answering. We can't hear you, *nyah, nyah*."
Maybe you screwed up, but it's unlikely you can fix this problem because you don't know its genesis. If the customer won't explain, let it go and move on.

"You screwed up, here's why." There's the gold; your customer is unhappy and willing to tell you why. Listen and analyze the problem. If you really screwed up, perhaps a late delivery or misinterpreted specification, learn from it, and fix the process that's broken.

But sometimes there's a different insight; you took on a customer or project that isn't right for you. You couldn't have done the job correctly, period. Do that too frequently and you're out of business.

Know your service and your market. Only accept projects (and customers) that are right for you. You can't be the best by delivering mediocre (or worse).

NEGATIVE SENTIMENT HAS THE POWER TO CHANGE THE WAY WE DO BUSINESS

When I received the following story in my inbox after sending out a HARO query[1] on the subject of negative feedback, it perfectly summed up the power of negative feedback. We all *think* we're capable of hearing things we don't want to hear about our brands and products—our children—but in reality, it's often a bigger punch to the gut than we imagined. Richard Hayman is the chief executive

---

[1] HARO is Help-a-Reporter Out[TM] (www.helpareporter.com), a website designed to bring together those looking for expertise (like journalists) and those who can provide it. If you're looking for a great way to share your expertise in a certain field and possibly drum up some press exposure for your brand, you should consider subscribing to their thrice-daily e-mail updates that will let you know who's looking for information you have to offer.

officer (CEO) of Hayman Systems (www.hayman.com), what started as a family-owned business and ended up being a national power-house in the cash register market. He explains how his company made a crucial shift, all thanks to one brutally honest customer:

> My father started his cash register business in 1938, and I joined the company in 1970. His customers became his friends and his friends became his customers. As his son, my clients were children of his clients. In some cases, my clients' grandfathers even did business with my grandfather.
>
> In the mid-1980s I was pitching one of our oldest and most loyal clients—a men's clothing store. I discovered that they had decided to take their business elsewhere, so I called to ask why. My client's words were concise, "I need a computer company, not a cash register company." You see, cash registers were first mechanical, then electronic, and finally, a combination of computer hardware and software. We were still in the mechanical phase, and that's not what our customers needed. I didn't need to hear that twice.
>
> Based on that one comment, we started our long journey of transforming our stodgy cash register company into a modern computer company. We learned very quickly that we had a number of challenges:
>
> 1. We couldn't train our existing staff on the new technology, plus we had thousands of older machines in place that needed service.
> 2. We didn't look or think like a computer company.
> 3. We were located in an older urban neighborhood and couldn't attract new talent. Even our customers were afraid to come to the office for training. We needed to move to a new building in an employment park.
> 4. We needed to change our name (at the time, we were Hayman Cash Register Company).
> 5. I was no longer the smartest guy in the company. I needed to hire people more knowledgeable than me.
> 6. We needed to reinvent ourselves to retain our existing customer base.

That's quite a list of to-dos, but we did it all. And we won an award in the mid-1990s for being one of Maryland's 50 fastest growing technology companies. The "fast growing" was OK, but becoming a *technology* company was real validation that we accomplished what we set out to do. Our main competitor, NCR, eventually became our supplier. We acquired additional locations and grew into one of the largest POS service companies in the nation. In 1999, we were acquired by our supplier, MICROS Systems (MCRS), who wanted to control more of their distribution.

For 61 years, our family business provided well for all of us. I was really lucky to have a friend who told me the truth. Being smart enough to listen made all the difference.

YOU COULD TELL THE NEGATIVE NINNYS TO %^* OFF, OR . . .

You could listen. Sometimes we all fall victim to our own good ideas, thinking no one else has value to add. *We've got this on lock down, and how dare you tell me I'm doing something wrong!?* But just think about what might (not) have happened if Richard Hayman and his father hadn't created a brand where his customers were comfortable giving him the brutally honest feedback he needed to point his business in the right direction. Narragansett Beer CEO Mark Hellendrung backs this up perfectly. "We don't pretend to be experts about everything. Our brand's critics and fans alike bring us some of the best ideas we've ever used to bring this brand to where it is today. It's amazing what happens when you listen and let people know you're listening."

Todd Bernhard is the president of No Tie, LLC, a developer for multiple best-selling smartphone apps, and takes listening one step further: he tracks down the people who are giving the negative feedback so that he can respond. The smartphone and mobile application marketplace is completely driven by user feedback and ratings; the more downloads and positive user reviews you get (all from anonymous users), the higher your app is ranked and the more visible it is to potential new customers. So how does a guy with more than

2 million completely anonymous users of his products deal with negative reviews that can have a detrimental effect on his business?

> As an app developer, one of the challenges is that I *don't* get direct feedback from the millions of anonymous people who use my apps. They buy from Apple, Google, and Microsoft and rarely reach out directly to developers. They're unaware that they can get better support for a $.99 app than a $99 software program. I've given out my cell number to users and walked them through the apps—try that with Bill Gates!
>
> One such user was in Alaska. I saw a negative review on iTunes App Store and was able to track her down and set up a call on Skype to see where she was having trouble. In the end, she changed her review to five stars!
>
> Not only does the negative feedback offer a chance to directly help a struggling user but it also tells me what areas of the app need improving as I roll out the next update.

Although you don't want to become a stalker, Todd's got the right idea. He's combined a great product offering with approachability and making sure that he continues to be profitable by servicing his audience to the best of his ability—even when (at first) he might not know the identity of the person leaving the negative feedback.

MEA CULPA = MAJOR OPPORTUNITY

There will come a day in the life of each of our businesses where we screw something up. It's the nature of the beast—we're building brands we want people to perceive as human, and humans screw up sometimes. How we choose to handle those screw-ups, however, is completely on us and goes back to the importance of creating a brand that makes people comfortable enough to tell us when we're not meeting expectations (or failed miserably). Without those conversations, we don't have the chance to make things right.

Shoplet (www.shoplet.com) is an online office supply retailer with no brick-and-mortar locations—and a Google rating of 4.5/5 stars calculated from more than 3,400 customer reviews. As a company that sells things and then ships them out, it's inevitable that they occasionally ship out the wrong item. The way they chose to deal with these situations put a smile on my face. Here's what Jeffrey Lustig, their head of marketing and development, had to share:

> Shoplet always looks at negative experiences as an opportunity to wow the customer. One of the ways we try to take advantage of these situations is by giving the customer more than they originally asked for. For example, when a Shoplet customer complains about being shipped the wrong item, we do more than just rectify what is clearly our mistake. What we *don't* do is ask the customer to go through the hassle of sending us back the wrong product once we've shipped the correct one. Instead, we suggest that the customer donate the incorrect item to the charity of their choice. This method for correcting orders has earned us enormous praise. Aside from completely satisfying the customer, we are able to work with them to turn this mistake into a positive experience for our customers' local communities.

Two wrongs can make rights—it just depends on how far you're willing to go to get to that right-hand turn. Shoplet demonstrates that it's possible to turn a mistake into something good and to have the good extend to more people than those who were even involved in the transaction initially.

POTENTIAL PERILS IN LISTENING TO NEGATIVE FEEDBACK

The businesses featured throughout this book offer overwhelming substantiation for listening to feedback and acting on it with a sense of logic and discretion, but having open ears can bite you in the ass sometimes. It's something that came up in my interviews with both Scott Rutherford, the cofounder of UserVoice, and Wendy Lea, the CEO of Get Satisfaction—the importance of evaluating feedback and deciding the best course of action (if there's any course to take at all) for your business.

Mark Frevert is the executive vice president of Grand Circle Travel (www.gct.com), a privately owned Boston-based tour operator offering travelers the opportunity to book trips around the world.

The company found itself in a game of Russian Roulette as a result of negative feedback, and the decision they made because of it nearly cost them a crucial segment of their 50-plus-year-old business.

> Grand Circle believes in cutting out products that don't meet its standards. Years ago, the Russia trip came up short on quality scores. A big problem was the food—travelers said it was awful, boring, and repetitive, with way too many potatoes. Another problem was that two of the senior leaders didn't really believe in the trip; they were concerned about the quality of the ship. Though GCC associates in Moscow and St. Petersburg said they were making progress, the product was cancelled. The big concern was that if the trip didn't meet expectations, the company would lose loyal travelers, which was too great a risk to take.
>
> It turned out to be a mistake. The quality scores for the final trip departures actually exceeded goals; however, it was too late to reverse the decision. The travelers were right all along—the food was boring—but that was a fixable issue that was addressed and improved. The decision to cut the trip was the result of acting too fast and failing to listen to the Russian associates. They were the ones who had the most current information and who really had their eyes and ears on the ground. It was a decision Grand Circle lived to regret, because it took an additional five years to get back into Russia. Acting on just the specific suggestions for improving the poor food could have rescued the entire product.

AND SO WE'VE COME FULL CIRCLE . . .

The importance of negative feedback to our respective brands is that it unveils the opportunities to do better business. Creating an unpopular brand—one that's invested in its audience, personality, approachability, sharability, and ability to provide exceptional value regardless of size and scope—opens the doors to that kind of feedback. You brought your audience inside and made them feel welcome, so there will be times they call our babies ugly. It might not be what we woke up that morning expecting to hear, but it's what we have to deal with to keep the cycle of unpopular going so that we can continue on this path we love.

Before we translate all of this into the next step—the ongoing care of our audiences and the power we as entrepreneurs provide for our local economies—let's have a look at this chapter's Case in Point.

Food and nutrition are touchy subjects, especially when part of your brand's value proposition is that your product will actually make people *feel better*. Brands like that naturally attract the skeptics, so let's see how the skeptics are good for GoodBelly.

CASE IN POINT: GOODBELLY

TURNING THE HATERS INTO LOVERS

Food, nutrition, supplements, and medication are all potentially volatile topics. There's always some yahoo lurking, ready and willing to tell you that what you're eating/taking is wrong and that you should be taking this whiz-bang, new-fangled snack. When you're a new brand coming onto the scene and you're trying to put what you believe in and sell into your audience's stomach, the snake oil salesmen of years past have cut your work out for you.

What if you're a brand that's really . . . good for you? How do you convey that message and deal with the folks who have been duped, conned, and failed by most other digestive health products they've tried? There's no better company to ask than GoodBelly Probiotic Juice Drinks out of Boulder, Colorado.

The mastermind behind the company is Steve Demos, a leader in the organic food movement and the one who brought Silk Soymilk into the dairy cases of mainstream grocery stores. When he sold his soymilk company, WhiteWave, Inc., to Dean Foods in 2002 the soymilk empire was valued at $296 million. After Demos left the company in 2005, a trip to Sweden proved just the catalyst to his next entrepreneurial pursuit, when Alan Murray, GoodBelly's current CEO, introduced him to a highly efficacious probiotic juice that was a staple in Swedish households. It was only a matter of time before he brought the highly treasured probiotic juice to this side of the ocean and named it GoodBelly.

GoodBelly is the only probiotic drink available in the United States that licenses the exact same probiotic strain (beneficial bacteria) that's available in the European product he discovered. In English? GoodBelly makes drinks that are good for your gut. In a time where food allergies and processed foods wreak havoc on our bellies, GoodBelly is (by design) actually *good* for you. And when you say things like that, people are ready and waiting to call bullshit on you. So how does GoodBelly deal with the haters? I had a conversation with Ariel Scott, the marketing voice for the product, and she filled me in on how they turn the frowns upside down.

Listen to the Skeptics

"We're in a health industry, making a product that we know will change the way a lot of our customers feel—and for the better," explains Ariel. "We run into skeptics quite often. They've had a long history of digestive issues, tried everything on the market, and just don't understand how we'll be any different from the rest of the world's offerings. And that's where the *Love it or it's FREE* GoodBelly 12-Day Challenge comes in."

Knowing full well that they're a start-up with limited resources, they don't go crazy with traditional marketing channels to spread the GoodBelly message. They're very active on Twitter and Facebook, and Ariel occasionally comes across the skeptics. The difference is in how they choose to handle these interactions.

"We could talk until we're blue in the face about the fact that GoodBelly can affect people profoundly, and like nothing else you've tried, but we came up with a *Love it or it's FREE* 12-Day Challenge so people could see for themselves, no matter how skeptical they first were. Love it after 12 days or it's free—how can you argue with that?" says Ariel. "The program includes e-mails with coupons, probiotics education, and personal
(continued)

(*continued*)

check-ins, and the response rate to my e-mails is astonishing. We can sometimes exchange 20 e-mails with one participant throughout the course of the trial. We are inundated with personal stories, questions, and requests. Keep in mind, many of these people were skeptics at first. All it took was for us to say, 'Hey—we're listening' to open the door to that skeptic to become a GoodBelly lover. People want to be heard, and we have a tremendous amount to learn from them. Our genuine desire to listen is a fundamental part of how we run our brand."

The trial period ends with a full money-back guarantee. Out of the thousands of people who participate in the challenge each month, the GoodBelly team processes just a few refunds—and happily. "If after having a 12-day trial and fully engaging with our brand someone doesn't love our product, at least they've given it a try. There will always be people who don't like us for some reason or another—our goal is just to have it never be because we weren't engaged with them."

Understand the Argument

Every business owner knows that some people just like to sound off, so how do you filter the ones who will never be happy out of the ones who you could potentially please? GoodBelly pays a great deal of attention to monitoring their brand across the social web, looking for reasons to reach out to anyone who's talking about them. They also have a high e-mail response rate to incoming messages about product sentiment. "The people who take the time to send us feedback on GoodBelly are people who are part, in most cases, of a passionate movement. They're passionate about nutrition, people with food allergies—people who are already invested in what our product stands for. If we chose to tune them out, we'd be making a terrible mistake. Every negative or potentially negative sentiment is our opportunity as a brand to create a positive outcome."

For example, GoodBelly is an organic, vegan, dairy- and soy-free product, but its entire line isn't gluten-free—at least not yet. With gluten-free lifestyles becoming more prevalent, they frequently receive messages from people who lambast them for not going the extra mile and taking the gluten out as well. Ariel and her colleague take the time to respond to every one of those inquiries, explaining why barley malt and oat flour (the culprits that make their product not gluten-free) are in their recipe. And then they do something else.

Whenever comments come across in a certain vein—gluten-free (GF), no added sugar, flavors—they categorize those people into lists. That way, when the product evolves to meet the needs of these people who hated that their needs weren't met, they can reach out to them when their product evolves to include GF. In 2010, GoodBelly launched their StraightShot product, which has no sugar added. Ariel reached out to everyone on that "no sugar added" list to let them know—"Hey! We listened!"

"Why listen if you're not going to do anything about it? Even the people who aren't currently happy because we're not meeting their needs have something to offer. In many cases, it's their ideas for a new product that we need to think about developing. I can't imagine why we'd ever tune that out." The StraightShot announcement received one of the highest response rates to an outbound e-mail yet—and it was all positive.

Negative Ideas = Solutions in the Making

Two tips that Ariel has for any business regarding dealing with the haters are:

- Figure out who's yelling and who's asking.
- Get in the pool with them.

Yelling vs. Asking

"Some people hate fruit juice. They're never going to like us in most cases. Other people don't like the smiley face on the top of our shots. When people are giving you negative feedback, you can do one of two things: put equal weight on everything

(continued)

(*continued*)

or sort it out. Sorting it out makes that feedback actionable. [So we try] to invest in our critics and offer them a way to become part of the solution."

Get in the Pool

"When you make your communications with the haters public and conduct yourself in a professional manner, people see that. Sure, there are plenty of things that you can deal with offline, and rightfully so, but something that's worked well for us is being as open and honest as possible. Odds are that other people are going to have the same question or concern, so if we can show we're not afraid to get asked and answer, that's one of the best brand decisions we can make."

We'll wrap GoodBelly's case study with a subject that riles all of us up: e-mail marketing. Every brand wants access to our inbox, and each of us goes on a <delete> spree multiple times a day. However, e-mail marketing has been one of the most successful branding and marketing efforts for GoodBelly to date. According to Ariel, "When we first started with our current survey company [SurveyGizmo], I would get calls and e-mails all the time with the same question: are your open and click-through rates a mistake? I'd laugh—baffled—and ask why. Apparently, the statistics on our campaigns are unheard of— nobody gets response rates like we do, and our highest rates are consistently when we ask the GoodBelly community to complete surveys so we can learn from them. Hey—we're just glad that people want to hear from us! It's an incredible compliment on how we've built the brand's voice and reputation."

GoodBelly Probiotic Juice Drinks
Boulder, Colorado
Website: www.goodbelly.com
Facebook: www.facebook.com/GoodBelly
Twitter: @GoodBellyDrink

CHAPTER 9

THE BACKYARD ECONOMY

A BIT ON NURTURING WHAT WE'VE BUILT . . .

I've built a brand based on unpopular thoughts and blunt advice, and the audience I've earned in the process is the single most important asset I have—and this will be true of the unpopular brand you're building, too. The best part about any audience is that they'll let us know when we're lacking and we'll love them for it.

What I've realized along the way is that I've done more than just build a brand—I've built a community. I've given these people who love what I create a place to hang out and other people to talk to. When I think about how I envision my community and the place I've created for them, I see a backyard. It's a place filled with conversations and laughter, shared interests, and great discourse. Sometimes, there's a brawl over in the corner between a couple of folks who had a little too much to drink, and there's always someone's kid chasing my dog around the yard. But no matter what's going on in my backyard, the most important thing is that my audience—my community—understands how much I value them and that I continue to invest in them.

I've invested in my Backyard Economy . . . so let's talk about *your* backyard.

UNPOPULAR BRANDS BUILD COMMUNITIES

The earlier pages that led you to this one are all about creating something for a specific audience and giving them a reason to come back to you and your solution. Unpopular brands—when built right—also build communities.

Yet, over time, we've built businesses in our local communities that, rather than supporting other businesses like our own, have gone the route of convenience—big-box retailers, massive supermarkets, anywhere we can get what we need in one place . . . and for less. We have the audacity to complain not only about where the U.S. economy sits but about the shape and texture of the global economy as well. And the kicker? Our behaviors in our own backyards don't even reflect the principles we've established while building our own brands.

I live in a state ripe with community and rich with innovation—and I've had to continually remind myself to shift focus back into my own backyard and think first how I can contribute here before I reach for what's convenient. What does your local community look like? I'll bet it's much the same—filled with people just like you who are starting and running businesses and who thrive on solutions. My community here in the Front Range of Colorado inspires me not only to be a better businessperson but also to determine how I can become a case study for living and feeding the Backyard Economy mentality. Your local community should do the same for you.

WHAT IS THE BACKYARD ECONOMY?

What boggles my mind as an entrepreneur is the feeling that we've somehow become a culture that wants to go *around* problems instead of work through them. Excuse me? We're entrepreneurs! We totally get off on working through problems. Yet despite the best laid plans, we've forgotten to translate the importance of these backyards we've built for our audiences—the places where we want them to live and breathe and exchange ideas—to the places where we ourselves live and breathe each day.

Businesses like ours are a significant part of our respective local economies. That's precisely why—after we've dedicated ourselves to traveling the unpopular path—we need to bring the focus we've given our brands to our immediate hyperlocal, local, and regional business ecosystems. It's another unpopular idea, and we're the ideal audience.

WHY YOU SHOULD CARE ABOUT THE BACKYARD ECONOMY

We can't turn on the television or tune in to the news without hearing about the state of the national economy across America, yet we're not the only global economy facing challenges, nor will we ever be. But what can we do as entrepreneurs and members of the communities we serve to ensure that we're cultivating a backyard—both locally and virtually—where audiences want to and *can* hang out? There are a few things we owe both to ourselves and to the audiences we serve and of which we're members. We'll talk first about how we can re-gain control of our Backyard Economies and then how to use the Backyard Economy mind-set to continuously monitor, nurture, and better serve our brands.

YESTERDAY, TODAY, AND WHAT WE CAN DO FOR TOMORROW

There was a time, one that many of us don't remember, where all economies were local. Technology hadn't evolved to the point where it is today, where we order everything from groceries to an automobile with a few clicks of a mouse. People walked to the butcher shop and ordered their meat in person; their clothes were made or altered by the local tailor. We knew our neighbors and what everyone in our town did for a living. Leaving our immediate neighborhood—*that* was a trip!

Time and technology have changed the world. Although we all may still need the same things, we go different places to get them. Local merchants have found themselves pushed out of business not only by the existence of one-stop-shopping superstores but also by the people who vote with their wallets by patronizing them. It's time to stop the diversionary tactics and finger-pointing about the state of our national economies and make it our job to change what we can in our own backyards. Just as we know that we're the only ones who can best serve our businesses, our brands, and their audiences, our local communities and Backyard Economies are the one thing we each have the power to change—and change now.

YOU'RE STILL A LOCAL BUSINESS

There's a lot of yelling that goes on when economies are out of whack. Those voices are necessary to start the conversations that drive needed changes. To be honest, it's easy to yell and express frustration—what's harder is finding ways to not only solve problems but also create environments where the future will be a more difficult place for an out-of-whack scenario to recur. As entrepreneurs, we're born problem solvers; we need to be responsible for the thought shift. We can rethink how we see our businesses, because regardless of your political belief system or the type of business you've decided to build, we are each building *local* businesses, whether you see yours as one or not. Even if your main business is one that lives online, check your backyard first.

We all live in hyperlocal, local, and regional community systems. Although you might serve a larger audience beyond borders you can reach by car in an hour or two, our respective businesses are still local. We pay local taxes in various forms and register our businesses with the state and county as required, and the revenue we generate goes to pay members of local communities—even if they're remote—and gives us the power to vote with our wallets and support other people who are just like us.

Even if we are dissatisfied with the state of our political system or economy, it is vital that we keep voting with our wallets. When you and I both paid more taxes than General Electric did in 2010 (net tax bill = $0), we are the ones who can bring that power back into our backyard by making better choices with where we spend our money. Here are three ways we can vote with our wallets, voices, and actions.

- **Support other local businesses.** It's a lesson worth learning from the start-up community. Places like Boulder, Colorado, and Silicon Valley produce more start-ups than anywhere else in the United States, and it has everything to do with the communities they build. Although everyone might be competing on some level for resources and investor dollars, they support one another. Why? Because they know if they don't, the community will disappear. The same, I think, has happened with local economies across the world; cheaper, more convenient solutions presented themselves, we grabbed them, and as a result, the importance we previously placed on local communities has faded.

  If you want your audience to support a local business like yours (which again, we are in some respect), spend your money with other local businesses. That means seeking out local vendors, skipping the big-box retailers when possible, and making the commitment to find other businesses just like yours that are following the unpopular path. Even if a business is beyond your immediate community, take a moment to learn a bit about it and whether you feel that spending your money with that company will help support a local economy other than your own.

- **Get involved.** Multiple case studies in this book address the value those companies found in getting involved in their local communities. There are so many people and organizations in need that one of the biggest decisions we have to make is where our business will focus its philanthropic efforts. Although we all run businesses that are looking to turn a profit, there is a place for charity and there are plenty of grassroots organizations that would be grateful for our commitment to their causes. When we support our Backyard Economies through philanthropy, we support the people throughout the communities where we rent office space, hire employees, do business, and pay taxes.

- **Practice brand philanthropy.** As entrepreneurs, we can help the voices of other businesses in our own backyards be heard— no matter where our respective business audiences live. We vote with our wallets and our time—and we can use the audiences we've cultivated to raise awareness for other businesses just like ours. It's brand philanthropy. And it's not about blindly supporting businesses because they're in your backyard. It's about finding the ones you can support through your own behaviors and experiences and sharing those far and wide from the rooftops— just as we'd like our audience do for us.

APPLYING THE BACKYARD ECONOMY TO OUR BRANDS

The Backyard Economy is still all about taking care of your audience. It just makes us realize that there are more people in our backyard than we might have originally thought and that supporting other businesses like ours allows us to regain control of something we didn't even know we'd given away. Our backyard requires maintenance. We have to keep it neat and the hedges trimmed, or people won't want to hang out there anymore.

Our brand's audience is its reason for being. Without it, the only thing you get to develop is the spread of your thighs on the couch of your choices and the only speaking you'll be doing is in front of imaginary audiences in your bathroom mirror.

The word *humility* has made multiple appearances throughout this book because I don't think it can be emphasized enough. By embracing our audience, we're able to stay humble, keeping *them* at the forefront of our attention and, consequently, doing a few things that other brands and businesspeople cannot.

- **Live in reality.** When we forget to care for our audience and recognize that they are our reason for being, we're off in some fantasy brand development world populated by mythical creatures and delusions of our own grandeur. The real world is the only place you can build a brand destined for survival because *your audience lives here.*
- **Cultivate a richer, healthier audience.** Followers, fans, Klout scores, Peer Index ratings, Yelp stars—we're all doing business in environments dominated by social rating systems. If I had a dollar for every potential client I've spoken with who wanted "5,000 fans in 30 days," I'd be able to give Charlie Sheen a run for his money in the Financing Hookers and Blow department. When we make our audience priority number one throughout the brand development process, we're able to build a more *meaningful* audience and with greater staying power than any brand—no matter what the comparative size—who thinks that collecting people and increasing numbers for number's own sake is the way to go.
- **Take care of your backyard.** That richer, healthier audience? We want them in our backyards. They are your most immediate Backyard Economy and the one that feeds our bottom lines. We built our brands by following an unpopular route by excluding while including, having an opinion, and becoming a part of people's lives—and all of these people feel comfortable enough to show up, relax, and hang out with us. The least we can do is take care of them and continuously reevaluate how we're doing in every aspect of creating the unpopular brand.

EMBRACE THE CYCLE

The easiest way to explain the importance of nurturing to brands is to put it in terms of a cycle. The five components of unpopular brands aren't hit-and-run techniques. If you think of them as a set of ideas that create a cycle, the care and feeding of our brands becomes a much more manageable process.

Although every sound business begins with a solution and then identification of the audience who will find that solution attractive, it doesn't end with reading the chapter on profitability and putting this book on the shelf. We have to let our businesses find their own rhythms as we travel the path of unpopular (as my screaming at you to pay attention to things won't help in the slightest). Some days we'll be more focused on approachability; others on scaling. The beauty of accepting our brand's development as a cycle is that we get to continually be amazed by its potential for evolution—and right alongside it, our own evolution as entrepreneurs.

WHAT THE PROPER CARE AND FEEDING OF OUR BACKYARD ECONOMIES YIELDS

It's as simple as this: we have a responsibility to take care of our communities. We can build a business that will become the next major national brand. We can even have aspirations to take that brand global. Maybe we're content with being the best eco-friendly dry cleaning service in our greater metropolitan area. Wherever our aspirations lie, we still have to take care of our Backyard Economies. No one's going to do it for us.

And if we, the people who thrive on improvement and change, don't step up and pave the path to better care and feeding for our backyards, our brand aspirations don't really matter a damn. Because if we're not taking care of our own, there's not going to be anyone left to invite to a barbeque in the backyards we love so much.

You never want to open your doors, day after day, and see an empty backyard. The reason we're each in business is because, for people like us, there is no alternative. We create solutions and feed them until they thrive. And as people who are prone toward solutions, we're just the right people to use our community-building skills to get things back on track. It's super unpopular to bear the responsibility for something greater than ourselves, but hey—that's who we are. Let's embrace our nature.

EPILOGUE: SHUTTING UP

I attended my twentieth high school reunion in Houston, Texas, two weeks prior to submitting this manuscript. Aside from the fact that it was 80 degrees and humid as hell—a stark contrast to having boarded a plane in a city where it was threatening the year's first snow—I partook in roughly 3 hours of reminiscing that yielded the following stats:

- Of the 360 people in our graduating class, barely 100 people showed up.
- The prom king and queen were conspicuously absent.
- My friends then were my friends now.
- Regardless of the glory of Facebook and its ability to broadcast our lives to the far reaches of the universe, I was asked repeatedly what I do. I responded that I'm a writer and own a marketing consulting company. The most popular responses were:
  - "Oh, that's neat."
  - "That's nice. Do you have kids?"
  - "Congratulations on becoming a writer!" (My personal favorite, as I didn't know there was an award for becoming a writer.)

It didn't matter what happened then versus where I'd brought my life to today. The people who cared were tuned in. And where I was able to bring my life to today had absolutely nothing to do with being perceived as "popular" by my peers.

That's the point.

We spend so much of our lives worrying about who likes us and what people think of us that we miss out on the most beautiful things along the way. We forget how much fun it is to wake up every morning and look at the people we love, say the things we need to say, and remember how fortunate we are to get to live our dreams. We could turn any random corner and bump into someone who hasn't found the bliss we live—if only we'd let ourselves live it.

I'd be a complete liar if I told you that this book turned out the way I had planned. The fans of my brand asked throughout the writing process when they'd be able to get a taste of my patented f-bomb-laced flavor of business wisdom. I started asking myself if f-bombs were necessary and if this was the place for them. Having read this you know, there's a lot of colorful language throughout the book, yet

191

the single trademark of my brand—the liberal use of the f-bomb—is scarce. And it's not because I thought about editing myself.

Part of building a successful brand lies in understanding how to introduce it to a variety of audiences so that they can take you or leave you. Josh from Freestyle Capital touched on this subject a bit—sometimes the ways we limit our brands make it hard for us to find the audience we need in order to make our passions a go. What I realized through the process of writing this book and interviewing all of the entrepreneurs who became the case studies you just read is there is no one single language that will apply to everyone, every time.

I'd gotten a healthy, mostly inadvertent dose of my own theory through my inadvertent omission of f-bombs. Stranger shit has happened to me (and you can take that to the bank).

Whatever the identifiers or hallmarks of the brands we choose to pursue, what remains important is that we leave the bullshit playground antics behind. They don't serve anyone, and all they'll ultimately do is keep you embroiled in some senseless and needlessly elitist routine that will alienate the people you need most to get your great ideas heard, loved, and shared. In business and life alike, we're entitled to nothing. We don't get cookies for having great ideas. Every day, we have to wake up and re-earn our place in the lives of the people who make it possible for us to do what we love. I think the best we can do each day is:

- Take a moment to humble ourselves. If it all went away tomorrow, what would remain? Never forget that people and relationships are what grant us access to life's greatest potential.
- Say thank you—often. And mean it.
- Make a commitment to help more people than we ask to help us.
- Have a reality check to see if we're content or actually complacent. One offers potential; the other's a pox.

Being unpopular puts us all in a hugely advantageous position in every facet of life. Unpopular brands strive to serve, love their audience, and are continuously committed to making them as much a part of their business as their audience makes their brand a part of their lives. They're humble and never forget that another player can come along at any moment and upset their tidy little apple cart, which is why they invest so much in nurturing the audience they've built. They ask tough questions and face tough answers, knowing that the outcome might not be what they envisioned but just what their brands needed.

But above all, unpopular brands are loved. Adored. Not by everyone and not by just anyone—but by the right people.

And the people who will never love them? Unpopular brands love them, too, because they're the leading reason we can build brands that last, are loved, and they make us glad to be a part of these brands each day when we wake up.

My greatest hope is that after you close this book, you're inspired to do something exceptional—in every facet of your life. Because when you draw the shades after a day well lived, it doesn't matter if you're popular. Embracing unpopular and all that it means is a braver path, and one that's a whole lot of fun. And based on all the data I have, we get to go around on this particular mortal coil but only once.

So if that's all we've got—one trip around—why don't we have some fun along the way and say to hell with anyone who thinks that they can stop us? Being unpopular means we get to wake up every day and live what we love.

Sounds like one helluva life, doesn't it?

Appendix A

Shit You Should Read, Who Wrote It, and Why

The following list of blogs and books aren't endorsements—paid or otherwise—for anyone's work. Rather, this is shit I actually read and have read. I've also included props to the authors and content creators as well as why each remains on my reading list. Much as I love them, lists are useless unless you put them in context. Since I'm not the only one out there with decent ideas, here are some other places you might find some good ideas for your life and business.

Blogs

A VC—Fred Wilson

www.avc.com (@fredwilson)

I spend a fair amount of time working with and covering the start-up community, so it would be pretty jerktastic if I ignored the venture capital community that goes hand in hand with it. We met Fred's blog briefly in Chapter 3 via FAKEGRIMLOCK, but more to the point, Fred's a principal at Union Square Ventures and a leading voice in the venture capital world. If you're running a start-up or work with them, his blog's a solid addition to your RSS reader or inbox for the latest trends and thought leadership in the start-up and venture capital/ funding world.

Jonathan Fields

www.jonathanfields.com (@jonathanfields)

I've been lucky enough to share conversations with Jonathan face to face, and those only make me love his blog more. I visit his blog for honest conversations and, above all, inspiration. Jonathan has the most peculiar knack for being able to turn a frown upside down without getting all ooey-gooey. His most recent book made the reading list in the next section as well. It's a must-read for anyone (read: all of us) who's ever experienced a failure to launch.

The Middle Finger Project—Ashley Ambirge

www.themiddlefingerproject.org (@TMFProject)

What do you get when you put a foul-mouthed writer with an entrepreneurial spirit in Chilé who just happens to be on the run from a whackjob ex-boyfriend? You get The Middle Finger Project. I love Ash and her in-your-face approach to getting you off your ass so that you can make things happen. Not a blog for those afraid of big, bad words and bold ideas.

Marketing Profs—Ann Handley

www.mpdailyfix.com (@marketingprofs)

Ann's the mastermind behind Marketing Profs, a site dedicated to delivering top-notch and timely information on marketing, branding, and current tech trends. The blog frequently features guest bloggers, and the voices vary. I love the diverse perspective. These are blogs you can e-mail to colleagues and coworkers and bookmark for future how-to reference. You can also check out MarketingProfs University (www.marketingprofsu.com), which offers tuition-based courses on assorted marketing materials. As a disclaimer, I was a paid instructor for these courses at the time this book was being written but was not encouraged to nor compensated for including this resource in the book, and I'm sure Ann will find it to be a pleasant surprise! It was a huge compliment to be invited to teach, as the reputation for their courses is well respected.

Start with Why—Simon Sinek

blog.startwithwhy.com (@simonsinek)

Simon's a more recent addition to my reading list. I was just introduced to him when I spoke at the SocialWyo conference in Cheyenne in October 2011. I love his blog because he asks tough questions and inspires tough decisions. He's frank and unassuming, yet this is a dude who knows his shit and can give an ass-kicking when I need one. If you ever asked yourself, "Why?" about anything, his blog and website itself (along with his book) could find their way to the top of your inspiration list. That's what he does—he inspires. It's also possible that his TED talk titled "How Great Leaders Inspire Action" is one of my all-time favorites, and I watch at least two TED talks a week. I find them to be the perfect antidote for bullshit.

BOOKS

The Alchemist—**Paulo Coelho**

It's a fable for adults about following your dreams and has sold millions of copies around the world. A personal training client of mine named Julietta originally gave it to me because she thought I needed to read it. The writing is simple; the messages strong. Sometimes you should be able to pick up a book and just . . . get it. This, to me, is one of those books.

The Entrepreneur Equation—**Carol Roth**

Every now and then, the right book comes along at just the right time. Carol sent me an advance copy of this book, and after letting it sit on my kitchen table for a few days because I was (apparently) too busy to give it a read, I tore through it in two days. Her book gives a clear, no bullshit picture of the realities of entrepreneurship. It's a concise guide that covers the homework you need to do and realities that need facing if you're going to build a brand that lasts.

Good to Great—Jim Collins

Occasionally, I have a major geek moment where only statistics, pie charts, and assorted and sundry data will satisfy. Although written back in 2001, Collins's profiles of multiple successful corporations and the hows behind why they surpassed similar companies in the marketplace will not only satisfy your inner geek but give you food for thought that can be applied to businesses of any scale. That, and I think hedgehogs are adorable, and he developed something he calls the Hedgehog Concept.

Killing Giants—Stephen Denny

Not only did Stephen Denny share his insights with me for this book, he has a book of his own that's beyond kick-ass. Jam-packed with case studies of hugely unpopular brands, *Killing Giants* continues where my case study on Mrs. G's in New Jersey left off—taking on your industry's giants and living to tell the tale. I am also desperately in love with the cover art and am delighted that my publisher liked the same color scheme.

The No Asshole Rule—Robert Sutton

If you're going to build an unpopular brand, you're going to run into assholes. Robert Sutton is just the guy to teach you how to deal with them. There are guidelines for employees and managers alike, along with lessons every entrepreneur can use to help him or her build a team worth having—and avoid becoming an asshole in the process of getting business done. Again, people are the world's most valuable asset, and just because some of them shit on us, it doesn't mean we have to put ourselves among them or be the recipients of such behavior.

Venture Deals: Be Smarter Than Your Lawyer and Venture Capitalist—Brad Feld and Jason Mendelson

The start-up industry has been starving for a definitive guide to term sheets, funding practices, and the mechanics that make this world go round. You won't find a more definitive guide in print, and it's well worth the price tag. Written by an attorney and lifelong VC, it's the double inside scoop on your start-up cone.

Winning the Customer—**Lou Imbriano and Elizabeth King**

If you're building a brand that requires the acquisition of new customers to stay afloat (umm . . . hullo?), this is probably the best 200-page read you'll have this year. Lou takes what he learned and implemented as the chief marketing officer of the New England Patriots and translates those concepts into actionable tasks for any business. The DELIVERS system described in the book is a keeper, too. What does that mean? Read it and find out—I'm not going to be the spoiler.

Uncertainty—**Jonathan Fields**

Do you ever wonder why we don't do all of those things we want to do? So did Jonathan Fields—so he researched it and wrote a book about it. There's not one of us who hasn't felt paralyzed by the uncertainty surrounding a particular decision. If you're looking for ways to change the fear into motivation, this is your book.

APPENDIX B

GETTING INTO IT—YOUR GUIDE TO RESOURCES ON THE BOOK'S WEBSITE

WWW.UNPOPULARBOOK.COM

As I promised at the beginning of this book, there are no workbooks included . . . mostly because I never liked homework. What I did instead is build a completely kick-ass website where readers can go not only to find information related to each chapter but to start and join in discussions with other entrepreneurs. We all get some of our best advice and ideas from others, so I created a place that will hopefully act as a catalyst for those discussions.

There are two tabs on the book's website you need to know about: Resources and Get Into It.

- **Resources:** This tab holds supplemental, and occasionally entertaining, information that supports each chapter. Just click on the chapter number and away you go! If you have any suggestions for things that should be added to the Resources for a particular chapter, you can post your suggestion in the Get Into It forum.
- **Get Into It:** Want to talk to me and/or other entrepreneurs about something in the book? Here's where you can do it. The entire forum is powered by Get Satisfaction, a company we met in Chapter 4. Each chapter of this book has a discussion thread set up so that you can navigate directly to that chapter and find or start conversations. Here's how to get started:
  - Click on the Get Into It tab on the website.
  - Select the chapter you want to discuss, ask a question regarding, offer praise for, etc.

- ○ Enter your question in the search box presented to see if there's already a discussion going on or if you'll be starting a new thread.
- ○ Go ahead and get into it!

There will be main threads set up for every chapter of the book beginning with Chapter 2, as well as one for Resources (where I mentioned you can make suggestions) and one for general questions that don't fall into one of the chapter headings.

And yes, every reader must either create a Get Satisfaction account or sign in using Facebook or Twitter authorization. There's no room for anonymous flamers or people who don't want to own their ideas. We're building a community, so we all need to get to know one another!